Cambridge Elements ☰

Elements in Politics and Society in East Asia
edited by
Erin Aeran Chung
Johns Hopkins University
Mary Alice Haddad
Wesleyan University
Benjamin L. Read
University of California, Santa Cruz

THE EAST ASIAN COVID-19 PARADOX

Yves Tiberghien
University of British Columbia

CAMBRIDGE
UNIVERSITY PRESS

CAMBRIDGE
UNIVERSITY PRESS

University Printing House, Cambridge CB2 8BS, United Kingdom

One Liberty Plaza, 20th Floor, New York, NY 10006, USA

477 Williamstown Road, Port Melbourne, VIC 3207, Australia

314–321, 3rd Floor, Plot 3, Splendor Forum, Jasola District Centre,
New Delhi – 110025, India

103 Penang Road, #05–06/07, Visioncrest Commercial, Singapore 238467

Cambridge University Press is part of the University of Cambridge.

It furthers the University's mission by disseminating knowledge in the pursuit of
education, learning, and research at the highest international levels of excellence.

www.cambridge.org
Information on this title: www.cambridge.org/9781108977913
DOI:10.1017/9781108973533

First published 2021

A catalogue record for this publication is available from the British Library.

ISBN 978-1-108-97791-3 Paperback
ISSN 2632-7368 (online)
ISSN 2632-735X (print)

The East Asian COVID-19 Paradox

Elements in Politics and Society in East Asia

DOI: 10.1017/9781108973533
First published online: July 2021

Yves Tiberghien
University of British Columbia
Author for correspondence: Yves Tiberghien, yves.tiberghien@ubc.ca

Abstract: The COVID-19 pandemic triggered the first global public health emergency since 1918, the greatest economic crisis since the Great Depression, and the greatest geopolitical tensions in decades. Global governance mechanisms failed. Yet in 2020, East Asian countries (with caveats) managed to control COVID-19 better than most other countries and to increase their cooperation toward economic integration, despite their position on the security front line. What explains this East Asian COVID paradox in a region devoid of strong regional institutions? This Element argues that high levels of institutional preparation, social cohesion, and global strategic reinforcement in a context of situational convergence explain the results. It relies on high-level interviews and case studies across the region.

Keywords: COVID-19, global governance, East Asia, regionalism, RCEP, China, Japan, Korea, Taiwan, ASEAN

ISBNs: 9781108977913 (PB), 9781108973533 (OC)
ISSNs: 2632-7368 (online), 2632-735X (print)

Contents

1 Introduction

Heralded by a benign cable report on the ProMED network of the International Society for Infectious Diseases on December 30, 2019, COVID-19 took humanity by storm and led to the greatest simultaneous lockdown in human history.

By May 4, 2021, the number of reported COVID-19 cases around the world reached 155 million, and the number of reported deaths passed 3.2 million. COVID-19 forced the highly sociable human species into isolation and rumination. It also led to a proliferation of nationalistic or subnationalistic responses, including the closure of borders and the appropriation of personal protective equipment (PPE), such as masks and respirators.

As countries around the world responded to the pandemic with massive quarantine and social-distancing measures, COVID-19 triggered the largest global economic shutdown in modern times and "the greatest economic crisis since the Great Depression," together with a massive social shock around the world. In the second quarter of 2020, economic activity decreased by a whopping 28% in Japan, 32% in the United States, and 39% in the Euro area.[1] COVID-19 also accelerated tensions among countries to dangerous levels, particularly between the USA and China. By shutting down global travel, transnational exchanges, and in-person summits, COVID-19 blunted diplomacy and brought world politics to the edge of a cliff.

COVID-19 marked the failure of early-warning systems in China and of pandemic preparations in most advanced countries around the world, except in East Asia. Most of all, COVID-19 will be remembered for the great gap between increased scientific advances and a poor public policy response in many leading countries of the West. Richard Horton, editor of leading medical journal *The Lancet*, writes:

> The global scientific community made an unrivalled contribution to establishing a reliable foundation of knowledge to guide the response to the SARS-COV-2 pandemic. And yet the management of COVID-19 represented, in many countries, the greatest science policy failure for a generation. (Horton, 2020: 41)

Pandemics can play havoc with cooperative intentions and institutions. They are great disruptors and agents of fragmentation. Pandemics have regularly reared their ugly heads throughout history and have had great impact on societies and nations. As we now know, the human species is literally coexisting with millions of unknown viruses ready for viral leaps from animals to humans.

---

[1] Source: Asian Development Bank. September 2020. *Asian Development Outlook 2020.* www.adb.org/sites/default/files/publication/635666/ado2020-update.pdf (last accessed November 23, 2020), p. 10.

Back in 1918–20, the great influenza epidemic (wrongly named the "Spanish Flu") killed between 50 and 100 million people worldwide, making it the greatest health disaster of the twentieth century (Arnold, 2018; Osterholm and Olshaker, 2020). The 1918 pandemic had a huge effect on the outcome of World War I by infecting German troops at the height of their Spring 1918 offensive. It forced an ailing British prime minister, David Lloyd George, into desperate isolation in Manchester for nine long days in October that year (Arnold, 2018: 209). The influenza also killed the prime minister of South Africa, the sociologist Max Weber, and Frederick Trump, grandfather of President Donald Trump (Barro et al., 2020). Several world leaders got sick during the Paris negotiations in 1919, including France's Prime Minister Georges Clemenceau and US President Woodrow Wilson (as well as the Spanish king and the German kaiser). The sickness weakened Wilson's energy and leadership in the negotiations of the Treaty of Versailles. In the wake of his own sickness (and the death of his grandson and daughter-in-law), as well as the death of 17 million across India, the pandemic also accelerated Gandhi's determination to fight for Indian freedom and launch the general strike movement in 1921 (Arnold, 2018: 209–210).

Research in behavioral psychology has documented the impact of pandemics on human cognition and human behavior (Taylor, 2019). Pandemics generate distrust and uncertainty; they have a disorienting and fragmenting effect. Medical expert Jonathan Quick writes that epidemics induce fear and that "we simply cannot think straight when we're fearful. We overreact. The Stone Age part of our brains, the amygdala, initiates a fear response and overrides the more rational frontal cortex; fears trump intellect" (Quick, 2018: 151). Using Kahneman's and Tversky's categories, pandemics intensify our emotional "system one" response and reduce the effectiveness of our more rational "system two" capabilities (Kahneman, 2011). They can threaten coordination within societies and cooperation among different countries.

It is, therefore, not a surprise that the global response to COVID-19 was fragmented and ineffective. This is especially the case given that COVID-19 hit humanity in the midst of a trade war and increasing security rivalry between great powers. Instead of encouraging restraint, leaders in key countries fanned the flames of uncertainty and fear in 2020 (Christakis, 2020). Throughout the year, cooperation among major countries was fractious, and peak leadership institutions failed. This includes the UN Security Council, the G20 Leaders' Summit, and the G7 (which did not even meet in 2020). Additionally, the US withdrawal from the World Health Organization (WHO) in the midst of the crisis seemed to mark the nadir of human cooperation. With President Biden's inauguration on January 20, 2021, and the immediate return of the USA to the

WHO, the wheels of cooperation began to turn again. But it took a long time and dramatic change within the United States.

Historians, though, may well remember 2020 as the year when East Asia tackled COVID-19 more effectively than Europe and North America and accelerated its rise as a result. The East Asian response to COVID-19 is the biggest surprise of the crisis.

The Dual Paradox of East Asia's Regional Response to COVID-19

This Element focuses on the national, regional, and global governance response to the pandemic in Asia, the initial ground zero of COVID-19. The virus arrived at a particularly bad time, with Asia already buffeted by disruptive American unilateralism, aggressive Chinese assertiveness, and escalating tit-for-tat tensions between them. As analyzed by Evelyn Goh, Asia was grappling with the buffeting forces of globalization and strategic rivalry in a complex economic-security nexus (Goh, 2020). Yet East Asia, despite its diverse political systems and stark security tensions, responded to the crisis with a combination of high performance and increased regional cooperation.

Punching above its Weight: East Asian Performance across Regime Types

The respective responses by East Asian and Oceanian countries to COVID-19 has been ranked the most competent on the planet. As shown in the following sections, even though COVID-19 started in Asia and there are significant differences among them, no East Asian nation is featured among the nations with the highest death ratio per capita. In global rankings of cumulated COVID-19 deaths per million inhabitants, results in early February 2021 ranged from a low of nearly zero (Vietnam) to a high of 2,500 in the state of New Jersey. The UK (second-highest country after Slovenia) stood at 1,650, Italy at 1,500, and the USA as a whole at 1,400. By contrast, nearly all East Asian and Pacific countries were found under 60 deaths per million residents as of February 8. The official results ranged from a high of 58 in Myanmar and 50 in Japan to a low of 0.4 in Vietnam and Taiwan, 1.1 in Thailand, and 3.3 in China. The two exceptions in this East Asian cluster were Indonesia (115) and the Philippines (101), which suffered from worse outcomes than the rest of the region but were still significantly below the world average (296).

As a result of early and effective health measures, East Asia has quickly weathered the economic shock and is on track to do better than any other region. According to the Asian Development Bank's April 2021 Development Outlook, Northeast Asia (not including Japan) is the only region that ended 2020 with a positive growth rate (+1.8%) and an expected 7.4% growth for 2021 (increased from the April, June, and September outlooks).[2] In January 2021, China announced that its total growth for 2020 reached 2.3%, after bouncing back to a 6.5% annual pace in the fourth quarter and surpassing expectations.[3] Japan took a larger hit with an expected −5.1% in 2020, to be followed by a slower recovery in 2021 (+3.1%).[4] Badly hurt by the collapse of tourism, Southeast Asia experienced more of a recession in 2020 (−4.0%) before expecting a bounce back in 2021 (+4.4%).[5] Vietnam, however, ended 2020 with a remarkable +2.9% growth rate and was on track for +6.7% in 2021.

The three best performers in the East Asian region during the COVID-19 shock in 2020 were Taiwan (+3.1),[6] Vietnam (+2.9%), and China (+2.3%).

By comparison, South Asia took a deeper hit (−6.0% in the region and −8.0% in India[7] for 2020), though it was expecting a large bounce back in 2021. However, two countries in South Asia finished 2020 with positive growth rates: Bangladesh (+5.2%) and Bhutan (+0.9%).[8] As a whole, the entire Asia and Pacific region (excluding Japan, Australia, and New Zealand) suffered only a mild hit of −0.2% in 2020 and could expect positive growth of +7.3% in 2021.[9]

Increased East Asian Cooperation under COVID-19

Most surprisingly, the East Asian response is also characterized by increased cooperation and increased regional integration. Clearly, this is the continuation of a preexisting trend. Nonetheless, COVID-19 seems to have driven home to Asian countries the urgency of cooperation as a way to survive the induced crisis. In the initial phase of the crisis in January–March, Japan and China shared PPE to a larger extent than European nations did with each other. And in spite of accrued security tensions between the United States and China and in China's periphery, Asian countries made orderly and rational decisions on global supply chains.

---

[2] Source: Asian Development Bank. April 2021. *Asian Development Outlook 2021*. www.adb.org /publications/asian-development-outlook-2021 (last accessed May 4, 2021).

[3] Source: *Nikkei Asia*. January 18, 2021. https://asia.nikkei.com/Economy/China-GDP-expands-2 .3-in-2020-with-fast-recovery-from-COVID.

[4] Source: International Monetary Fund, January 26, 2021. *World Economic Outlook: Update.*

[5] Source: Asian Development Bank, April 2021, *Asian Development Outlook.*

[6] Source: ADB, April 2021 and *Nikkei Asia*. January 29, 2021. https://asia.nikkei.com/Economy/ Taiwan-GDP-growth-outpaces-China-for-first-time-in-three-decades.

[7] Source: ADB, April 2021 and International Monetary Fund, January 26, 2021. *World Economic Outlook: Update.*

[8] Source: Asian Development Bank, April 2021, *Asian Development Outlook.*

[9] Source: Asian Development Bank, April 2021, *Asian Development Outlook.*

The health, economic, and geopolitical triple shock brought on by COVID-19 in 2020 was a crucial test for East Asian regionalism. It was the first critical global crisis since 1990 in which systemically important countries could not agree to cooperate. It was also the first major crisis in which the leader of the global system, the United States, actively worked to undermine key pillars of the multilateral global order. This put a tremendous burden on informal and regional institutions, adding to the growing strains of power shifts.

Asia entered the COVID-19 maelstrom with a deficiency in robust regional institutions, relying instead on "soft institutionalization." Unlike the European Union, Asia has not matched its growing economic interdependence with layers of institutions and organizations. The two most powerful countries in East Asia, China and Japan, have not been able to come to an understanding on how the region should be governed, in great contrast to the Franco-German partnership in Europe. Instead and counterintuitively, it is the Association of Southeast Asian Nations (ASEAN), with its ten members, that led Asian institution-building. "Soft institutionalization" is essentially the partial generalization of the ASEAN way to the rest of Asia. It is defined as "organizational minimalism, the avoidance of legalism, and an emphasis on consultations and consensus decision-making" (Khong and Nesadurai, 2007: 11). This regional approach embeds a "high degree of autonomy for governments in their domestic policy" (Khong and Nesadurai, 2007: 78). It has long been seen as limited and fragile, especially in the context of the great diversity in regime types and historical legacies in the region. And for all their innovation, ASEAN countries cannot really call the shots. Ultimately, China, Japan, the United States, and (increasingly) India are the true heavyweights in the region. Under the COVID-19 shock and with escalating tensions among the great players, one could expect great damage to the informal institutions of East Asia.

Lo and behold, the region did not fall into the COVID-19 conflict trap. No development exemplifies the Asian response more than the signing of the Regional Comprehensive Economic Partnership (RCEP) on November 15, 2020, in Hanoi, after eight years of arduous negotiations. Achieving the largest free trade agreement in the world in the midst of security tensions and a great pandemic is counterintuitive to say the least. In one bold move, fifteen East Asia and Pacific nations – representing 30% of the world's population and an equal share of the global economy – inked a regionwide accord and buttressed supply chains among them, with China at the core. India did not join, but the fifteen signatories left a special door open welcoming India to do so at any time in the future. And there is no doubt that key RCEP members such as Japan, Korea, Singapore, and Malaysia will seek to enhance their existing bilateral agreements with India instead.

Even though most RCEP partners outside China are greatly concerned about China's recent political and security moves, particularly in Southeast Asia (Emmerson, 2020; Strangio, 2020; Hiebert, 2020b), it is hard to exaggerate the signal sent by the conclusion of the RCEP in the midst of the COVID-19 catastrophe. It symbolizes a degree of convergence and understanding within Asia about response to COVID-19, support for globalization, and belief in multilateralism, whatever the security and political tensions. It also marks the realization in East Asia outside China that decoupling from China is geographically and economically impossible and that it is wiser to build more institutionalized and regularized economic links in response to higher tensions.

East Asia is not the only region that turned the COVID-19 lemon into an opportunity for increased cooperation. Africa managed to develop a coordinated response to the crisis and to keep its project of an African free trade area on track. The European Union made several breakthroughs, including a jointly financed recovery plan that involves the first jointly issued bonds for the sake of fiscal transfers to badly hurt regions and a strong common stance in Brexit negotiations. On December 30, the EU also finished the year 2020 with a daring Comprehensive Agreement on Investments (CAI) with China, after China made a series of significant last-minute concessions to the EU to seal the deal. The CAI may have represented one of the key geopolitical developments of 2020, along with the RCEP, even though the path to ratification appeared very difficult within the EU, especially after the tit-for-tat sanctions over Xinjiang that took place in March 2021. This study focuses on East Asian developments but has implications for these other regional advances in 2020.

To sum up, this Element focuses on two core puzzles. First, what explains East Asian over-performance in the COVID-19 crisis? And second, why did East Asian nations manage to cooperate and accelerate regional integration in the midst of COVID-19, while global multilateralism faltered?

Why the Asian COVID-19 Puzzle Matters

Understanding the institutional and policy drivers that enabled most East Asian countries to beat COVID-19 and save their economies greatly matters for the rest of the world. What can we learn? Can some of the East Asian policy innovations travel beyond the region to help prepare for future pandemics?

This Element also argues that the COVID-19 crisis offers a useful prism to revisit the comparative analysis of the East Asian regional system. Given its lack of institutions to match its deep liberal integration, East Asian regionalism is seen as weak, crippled by political regime divergence and highly reliant on the US anchor as market of last resort and security provider. The regional literature has identified corporate and human networks (initially Japanese, then also Korean) as a key element of robustness (Katzenstein and Shiraishi, 1997; Pempel, 2005; Calder and Fukuyama, 2008; Calder and Ye, 2010).

Theoretically, a loosely institutionalized region would seem more liable to fragmentation. Cooperation under loose coupling, conflicting political values, disconnected media bubbles, and extremely diverse levels of development and institutional capacity is very hard indeed. In this sense, East Asia offers a good test case for the survival of civilization under global disruptions. What are the greater lessons for humanity? When humans are separated by core narratives, how can they still cooperate against a common threat?

As well, this puzzle may help us rethink the question of regional institutional resilience. Flexible and inclusive regional arrangements without clear breaking points and rigid rules may be less vulnerable in times of crisis.

Empirically, cooperative capacity in Asia matters, since Asia is at the heart of the global economy, with 60% of world growth expected to come from the whole Asian region. It is also the main battleground for the most intense political rivalry, that between China and the United States.

The literature offers several possible answers to the East Asian COVID-19 paradox. First of all, East Asian cooperation could be seen as the embodiment of liberal resilience in general. Ikenberry argued that the Liberal International Order (LIO) orchestrated by the United States after 1945 is resilient and flexible enough to be attractive to emerging powers and to deal with crises (Ikenberry, 2011). The East Asian region could be the arena for a replay of a collective liberal effort to save the system, just as G20 nations did in the wake of the 2008 Financial Crisis (Drezner, 2014). What remains puzzling, however, is the fact that the LIO in 2020 was stretched to the limit (Ikenberry, 2018) and its architect, the United States, actively worked against its core pillars.

Realism might offer an alternative explanation: indeed, the East Asian states neighboring China may choose to increase regional cooperation as a way to bandwagon with a rising China. More convincingly, they may pursue a hedging strategy, whereby they combine economic cooperation with China with participation in US-led security alliances aimed at deterring China (Kuik, 2020; Kuik, 2008). However, strategic hedging is exceedingly hard to pursue collectively across a very diverse region through institutional advancement.

A third plausible explanation might focus on leadership. In his path-breaking study on global collective goods, Barrett argued that leadership by key states is essential. "The important point is this: when the opportunities to supply a global public good are seized by the great powers, motivated only by self-interest, but acting 'within the framework of the general good,' the entire world benefits" (Barrett, 2007: 11). In the case of the Asian response to COVID-19, one would particularly look to China and Japan as providers of key public goods. Japan under Prime Minister Shinzo Abe has indeed increased its leadership in the global order (Tiberghien et al., 2020). Yet Asian developments in 2020 have not supported the advance of a feared Chinese hegemony. The process appears much more diffuse. The RCEP was led by ASEAN. Furthermore, key Chinese actions throughout 2020 – such as its "wolf warrior" diplomacy, aggressive moves in the South China Sea or in the border area with India, and threats to Taiwan – have not been conducive to its winning acceptance as a leader in the Asian region (Rudd, 2020).

The Argument: Institutional Capacity, Social Cohesion, and Global Strategic Reinforcement

To explain the puzzle of high performance in most of the region, this study advances an institutional approach that emphasizes preexisting centralized governance structures. These institutions operate one level below the political regime itself and cut across regime types. They are situated one level above the health-care delivery institutions, the quality of which varies from extremely high in Japan to low in Myanmar and the Philippines. Whether autocracies or democracies, most East Asian states are Weberian in their heart: they believe in modern bureaucratic institutions to sustain free markets, solve market failures, and distribute economic gains (World Bank, 1993). They believe in progress through institution building. Most countries had established universalistic health systems (with great variations, of course, according to levels of development, and with lower levels in countries such as Cambodia, Indonesia, Myanmar, or the Philippines) prior to the pandemic and accepted the role of government to provide collective security in times of crisis. These conditions are not sufficient in themselves, as was shown in many European countries during the pandemic, but they are necessary.

Again with caveats for the cases of Indonesia and the Philippines, nearly all East Asian cases had put in place laws, centers for disease control, and response procedures prior to the pandemic. To staff these institutions, most East Asian countries developed highly skilled human capital and trained a cadre of disease specialists. Practically everywhere, governments relied on those structures led by respected scientists to set the policy response.

Initially, the Chinese local government in Wuhan silenced its scientists and overrode its health procedures for the sake of political expediency, with serious global consequences. Yet China's central leadership eventually swung back to full reliance on its medical experts and medical bureaucracy after January 20, with great effect.

This parallel Weberian response in nearly all East Asian cases had roots in each political system – notwithstanding variation according to their respective developmental modernization processes. However, the convergence and similarities are striking. For all its lack of hard institutions, the region did benefit from common drivers that may have reinforced national trajectories. Japan's early success in industrialization, followed by the success of East Asian "tigers" and eventually of China, reinforced a competitive dynamic toward adoption of state institutions that seemed to perform well. In addition, Japan itself played a key role in developing health governance in Southeast Asia and beyond, either directly or through the Asian Development Bank. Norms and practices travelled across the region in a process of mutual reinforcement. Health scientists across the region knew each other and cooperated closely together, including Taiwanese and mainland Chinese scientists for example. SARS in 2003 also played an accelerator role as a common shock, especially in Hong Kong, Singapore, Vietnam, and Taiwan, while Korea responded more to MERS in 2009.

Second, this Element argues that the government response in East Asia was able to rely on high levels of social cohesion and social trust in times of common peril. Surveys on social cohesion and social trust consistently put East Asian cases, such as China, Singapore, and Indonesia, near the top alongside India, New Zealand, Australia, and the Nordic countries. Across the region, citizens mostly followed social norms such as mask-wearing and physical distancing. New Zealand and Australia benefited from high levels of social trust along with institutional capacity and personal leadership (in the case of Prime Minister Jacinda Adern).

Regarding the puzzle of increased regional cooperation, this study argues that this was the result of global strategic reinforcement in the face of situational convergence. In a time of crisis, policymakers in the region doubled down on what worked before: increased trade and regional integration supported by advances in rulemaking. This was a strategic response to a situation of global uncertainty – a flight to safety, of sorts. With its high dependence on trade, the region is most vulnerable to the erosion of globalization and the liberal international order. Facing growing dangers in the middle of a trade war, East Asian leaders reasserted their commitment to regional interdependence and resisted decoupling.

This response may have been facilitated by the outcome of our first puzzle, namely the fact that all East Asian countries responded with similar reliance on institutions and scientific expertise, despite differences in levels of transparency and privacy protection. Competence breeds trust among similar bureaucracies.

The increase in security tensions and political risks in the region echoes strongly within security communities in the region and with public opinion. Yet, given the presence of China at the heart of the region, the responses of countries such as Japan, Korea, Australia, and Singapore entail developing competent security responses as part of their alliance with the United States, while seeking to institutionalize economic relations with China. In 2020, security tensions did not overwhelm the trading logic. This response of US allies in East Asia also builds upon long-held norms of political noninterference and forbearance in a long-term perspective. Building on histories of interactions with China going back centuries, these neighboring countries have a tendency toward pragmatic management. They have a sense of the deeper drivers of Chinese governance beyond the particularities of the current leader. They know that they cannot escape China's massive orbit without unbearable costs to their economy and living standards. In the short term, the pandemic shock in the context of the US-led erosion of global institutions reinforced the need for regional stabilization.

There are two important caveats. First, the attempt of the region to link with India failed in the case of the RCEP, and economic connectivity between South Asia and East Asia remains a work in progress. Second, the relentless rise and often arrogant attitude of China in the region represents a shared concern. The region remains highly vulnerable to either unilateral Chinese moves or harsh tit-for-tat sequences between the USA and China, even under the Biden administration. A security crisis could overwhelm regional institutions. This Element shows, however, that, below such security tensions, shared norms and economic institutions remain resilient. They offer a strong counter narrative to high political drama that dominates the airwaves.

Methodology and Roadmap

This Element relies on a variety of sources and methods. It employs the comparative method to study convergence and coordination among very distinct countries with a great diversity of regime types and levels of development. It also employs process-tracing to unpack the drivers of key decisions, such as the RCEP, for key countries such as Japan. I make use of both quantitative data sets and qualitative analyses of individual countries. I also use personal interviews with decision-makers in Asia between December 2018 and December 2019, as well as digital interviews and public speeches by key actors during 2020.

The Element proceeds through five sections.

Section 2 presents the global setting for the COVID-19 crisis and argues that the global governance response mostly failed in 2020, leaving a greater burden to carry at the regional and national levels.

Section 3 focuses on domestic governance and compares COVID-19 performance within Asia and in contrast to other regions. It advances a list of key causal factors to explain such performance across political regime types, including the presence of common principles and narratives in the study of key country cases in the region.

Section 4 focuses on resilience at the regional level, in particular the China–Japan relation, the roles played by the AIIB and the ADB, and the logic behind the conclusion of the RCEP.

The conclusion derives long-term lessons and implications from this pivotal set of events.

2 COVID-19, Triple Shock, and Failure of Global Governance

> Humanity needs to make a choice. Will we travel down the route of disunity, or will we adopt the path of global solidarity? If we choose disunity, this will not only prolong the crisis, but will probably result in even worse catastrophes in the future. If we choose global solidarity, it will be a victory not only against the coronavirus, but against all future epidemics and crises that might assail humankind in the 21st century.
>
> (Harari, 2020)

COVID-19 is a tiny virus that most likely originated from a humble bat somewhere in China and somehow made a leap to a human, despite lingering questions about its origins.[10] It was just one among many viruses that exist within the animal kingdom around the planet. This coronavirus somehow ended up in the midst of a huge global metropolis, Wuhan, on the eve of the great Chinese New Year migration and spread far and wide. The local government in Wuhan initially failed to recognize its potency after COVID-19 was identified on December 30, 2019, and decided to instruct doctors to be quiet about it, while focusing on political stability. In a tragic decision, Wuhan leaders put the priority on holding the routine annual political Congresses, instead of switching to full emergency mode. The Wuhan Municipal People's Congress met as scheduled over five days, January 6–11, bringing together the city's entire top leadership.[11] All medical announcements stopped during that time. This was followed by the annual meeting of the full People's Congress of Hubei Province on January 12–17 and a long-planned giant banquet with 40,000 guests on January 18. During part of

---

[10] Two leading Chinese scientists have argued in the highly respected journal *Science* that the exact original location of the initial outbreak of COVID-19 remains unknown. They also argue that "meat from SARS-CoV-2–infected animals or food packaging contaminated by SARS-CoV-2 could be a source of human infection." See Zhou P and Shi Z-L (2021) "SARS-CoV-2 spillover events," *Science* 371(6525): 120. Most international scientists see these hypotheses as extremely unlikely. Others have raised the possibility of lab leak.

[11] Source: Susan Lawrence. May 11, 2020. "COVID-19 and China: A Chronology of Events (December 2019-January 2020). Congress Research Services Report # R46354. Available from: https://crsreports.congress.gov/product/pdf/r/r46354, p. 23.

this time, Xi Jinping himself was travelling away from Beijing in Myanmar and remote areas in Yunnan (January 17–19) on long-planned trips.[12]

On January 20, however, the Chinese central government switched to emergency mode and essentially took over, announcing the presence of human-to-human transmission and ordering a quarantine of Wuhan (effective January 23). After January 23, China managed to control and defeat COVID-19 within its territory with sweeping measures, but the virus had escaped beyond its borders. It soon became a global pandemic.

Because it combines the ability to spread easily (medium-high R0 index) with the cunning ability to stay invisible among its human hosts for days and spread between asymptomatic patients, while still killing 1% to 2% of symptomatic patients, COVID-19 triggered massive countermeasures everywhere. By March 2020, most countries in the world unveiled measures of quarantine or physical distancing. The global walking mobility index had dropped by 70% and the global driving index by 60%.[13] This happened overnight. In April, air traffic at Heathrow Airport in London was down 97%.[14] Observing such incredible changes happening in the blink of an eye, Yuval Harari wrote: "Decisions that in normal times could take years of deliberation are passed in a matter of hours. Immature and even dangerous technologies are pressed into service, because the risks of doing nothing are bigger. Entire countries serve as guinea-pigs in large-scale social experiments" (Harari, 2020).

COVID-19 has been called the greatest global public health crisis since the influenza outbreak of 1918. It turned out that many countries were not ready for it, including leading nations such as the United States and the United Kingdom. Yet the massive measures taken to deal with the coronavirus generated a secondary global shock through the voluntary shutdown of a quarter to a third of the global economy: the "greatest crisis since the Great Depression," in the words of Gita Gopinath, chief economist at the International Monetary Fund.[15] Economist Paul Krugman called it a "medically induced coma."[16] And it quickly generated a massive social and moral crisis, as the costs of the pandemic and of the

---

[12] Source: *Nikkei Asia*. January 14, 2021. "Analysis: Photo in Xi's office holds secret to COVID probe resistance. China's leader was absent from Beijing in the initial days of the pandemic." https://asia.nikkei.com/Editor-s-Picks/China-up-close/Analysis-Photo-in-Xi-s-office-holds-secret-to-COVID-probe-resistance (last accessed February 8, 2021).

[13] Source: International Monetary Fund. October 2020. *World Economic Outlook: A Long and Difficult Ascent*. p. 44, based on Apple Mobility Index.

[14] Source: *Financial Times*. www.ft.com/content/2bcfd765-8ded-412a-9493-2144020d863d?shareType=nongift.

[15] Source: Gita Gopinath. October 13, 2020. IMF Blog. https://blogs.imf.org/2020/10/13/a-long-uneven-and-uncertain-ascent/.

[16] Source: *Business Insider* interview. March 31, 2020. www.businessinsider.com/paul-krugman-us-economy-coma-coronavirus-more-fiscal-aid-2020-3.

economic stoppage disproportionately hit service and frontline workers, women, people of color, poor people, and disadvantaged groups around the globe.

Unlike in 2008 with the Global Financial Crisis or 2009 with the H1N1 virus, leading nations of the world failed to develop a common response, both to the pandemic and to the economic crisis. Global institutions such as the UN Security Council, the G7, and the G20 failed, as the USA turned against them and the USA and China engaged in high-voltage confrontations. Global institutions such as the WHO came under attack. The health and economic shocks deepened the security and political rifts that had arisen in the years leading to 2020. As leading countries came to blows, COVID-19 triggered a crisis of global governance and geopolitics. The fog of the pandemic gave cover for aggressive moves by opportunistic nations, and conflicts multiplied.

Thus, in a mere couple of months, COVID-19 set off a triple global conflagration affecting global health, global economic and social well-being, and geopolitics.

The Health Shock: Collective Failure of Pandemic Control

When we contemplate the immense damage wrought by COVID-19, the most amazing observation is that health scientists had clearly raised the alarm ahead of time. In their 2017 book, Dr. Michael Osterholm – the epidemiologist directing the Center for Infectious Disease Research and Policy (CIDRAP) at the University of Minnesota, and now a member of the Biden COVID-19 taskforce – and author Mark Olshaker warned that influenza pandemics and coronavirus pandemics were extremely likely to hit humanity in short order. Indeed, they represent the two most dangerous pandemic threats to humanity (Osterholm and Olshaker, 2017). They also singled out the two most dangerous conveyor belts for germ invasion: bat colonies in many tropical regions and chicken and pig factory farms acting as incubators of coronaviruses and influenza strands, respectively. With respect to pigs, they noted: "They can become infected with both avian influenza viruses and human influenza viruses simultaneously, and their lungs provide an ideal mixing bowl" (267).

Dr. Megan Murray at Harvard Medical School has studied the lessons of many past pandemics, including the 1910–11 plague that originated in Harbin (transmitted through a small marmot). She concludes that "many emerging diseases are zoonotics that emerge at the boundary of wilderness and human life" and that human mobility then spreads the disease.[17] Pandemics always hit the poor and vulnerable hardest. "Diseases thrive at fault lines of society."

---

[17] Source: Remarks by Doctor Megan Murray at the online event hosted by Harvard Medical School and MassCPR as part of Worldwide Week at Harvard on October 7, 2020, and titled "Global Perspectives on COVID-19."

Remarkably, Osterholm and Olshaker offered a scenario for an influenza-like pandemic originating in Shanghai, China, that would spread from people to people through breathing and would lead to struggles over masks, respirators, and vaccines, along with a great global crisis. They warned: "We live in a globally interdependent world, with widespread rapid travel and many concentrations of people, pigs, and birds living in close proximity. Thus, that world has become a hypermixing vessel – one with about three times the human population of 1918" (Osterholm and Olshaker, 2017: 268). The two authors correctly predicted a catastrophic pandemic "will unfold like a slow-motion tsunami, lasting six to eighteen months" (269). These and other warnings went unheeded.

In their 2020 edition, Osterholm and Olshaker wryly note that pandemics like COVID-19 always end up coming as a surprise when they shouldn't. "Nor should the next one; and rest assured, there will be a next one, and one after that, and on and on" (Osterholm and Olshaker, 2020: xvii). In his 2018 book, Jonathan Quick concurs that deadly pandemics will originate from both the bush (as in the cases of Ebola, AIDS, and Zika) and the barn (influenza strands like H1N1). For example, the H1N1 epidemic of 2009 that killed almost 600,000 people and created a costly global crisis originated in pig farms in North Carolina and transited through a massive 60,000-sow factory farm run by Smithfield Foods in Mexico (Quick, 2018: 50). Quick also predicted the "ricochet effect" of pandemic spread through airplane travel around the globe, as well as the ensuing "aversion behavior and epidemic cascade" (80–81).

In short, coronavirus or influenza pandemics are waiting to happen. The proximity of new megacities to both jungles and farms, as well as globally connected airports means that the risk of pandemics keeps rising. And yet our preparedness and health governance system failed in the case of COVID-19, both at the national levels (in most countries, but not all, as shown in Section 3) and at the global level.

Three partial failures stand out in the battle to stem the spread of COVID-19 around the globe. The first is the failure to rapidly identify and contain COVID-19 at the source by Wuhan authorities in December 2019 and January 2020. At the heart of great international tensions, this point has become highly sensitive, and much is yet unknown about the exact sequence of events from a bat to humans that led to the COVID-19 explosion. Based on available information to date, it is possible to offer a mixed diagnostic: China made noted improvements compared to its handling of the SARS virus. Yet, there were also significant gaps in initial control and timely information-sharing.

Clearly medical expertise in China has dramatically improved since the situation in 2003 during the SARS epidemic. Doctors in Wuhan raised the alarm about suspected person-to-person transmission of the mysterious new pneumonia as early as December. The first such instance known took place on December 27, when Dr. Zhang Jixian of the Hubei Provincial Hospital of Integrated Chinese and Western Medicine reported a suspicious family cluster to her superiors.[18] On December 30, ophthalmologist Li Wenliang exchanged messages with colleagues about the transmission of this new SARS-like pneumonia.

Most importantly, Chinese scientists managed to identify and determine the genetic sequence of the new virus by January 10, a historic breakthrough. They shared it with the world on January 11. Prof. Zhang Yong-Zhen at Fudan University was the first to post the genetic sequence of the virus on open-access platform Virological.org. China CDC and two other teams followed, posting genetic sequences on Global Initiative on Sharing All Influenza Data (GISAID), another open-access platform, and with the WHO.[19] This sequence enabled disease control centers and biotech companies around the world to create test kits within January (for the fastest countries) and to start the race for a vaccine.

However, precious time passed between the identification of the first cases in early December and the notification to the world on December 31 through the ProMed platform. It is plausible that December was dominated by uncertainty and unknowns. Horton himself asks: "Did local Communist Party officials suppress evidence of a new virus?" (Horton, 2020: 19). Pending the results of ongoing investigation, the answer is probably yes. We may add two more questions. Was there also genuine confusion about the situation and genuine concern about triggering panic among the population without full information? Probably yes. Did the Wuhan authorities fully inform central authorities in Beijing? Probably not. The March 30, 2021, WHO investigation (co-led with Chinese scientists) provided much useful information but eventually could not answer these questions.

The 2005 International Health Regulations (IHR) of the WHO require countries to notify the WHO within twenty-four hours of any new public health emergency. Yet, the available timelines indicate no information was transmitted in December. China sent an official report to the WHO only on January 4, even though the WHO had sent an official request for information on December 31. Information on human-to-human transmission seems to have reached the WHO

---

[18] Source: Susan Lawrence. May 11, 2020. "COVID-19 and China: A Chronology of Events (December 2019–January 2020)." Congress Research Services Report # R46354. Available from: https://crsreports.congress.gov/product/pdf/r/r46354, p. 9. This has also been publicly confirmed by Dr. Zhong Nan Shan.

[19] Source: Susan Lawrence. May 11, 2020. "COVID-19 and China: A Chronology of Events (December 2019–January 2020)." Congress Research Services Report # R46354. Available from: https://crsreports.congress.gov/product/pdf/r/r46354.

informally only on January 14 and formally on January 20.[20] This delay in providing critical information, possibly caused by central–local transmission failures and by political intervention, has caused great friction between China and the USA, as well as with other countries. Significant delay also took place before the WHO could dispatch an early inspection team to China and Wuhan in February. Prevarication happened again in November and December, when the WHO could not get authorizations for its formal investigation team on the origins of COVID-19 to travel to Wuhan. The go-ahead finally came in January 2021.

Additionally, between December 31, 2019, and January 20, 2020, the Wuhan authorities were involved in reprimanding doctors such as Li Wenliang, who sought to alert his colleagues to the dangerous new virus. In so doing, the local government blocked the spread of information on the spread of the disease and prioritized holding long-planned large local events instead.

Full information came only on January 20, after Beijing dispatched a team of six national experts headed by Dr. Zhong Nan Shan, the hero of SARS, for a hard-headed investigation. After a deliberation process balancing the pros and cons of mitigation versus suppression strategies, it was decided to focus on saving human lives and implement "an intensive suppression strategy."[21] Wuhan established an epidemic prevention and control command center. A complete lockdown of Wuhan followed on January 23 and of the province of Hubei (with 60 million people) a couple days later. But millions of people had already left Wuhan for the great Chinese New Year holiday trek. By early February, Beijing sent an inspection team and replaced the Party Secretary and other key members of the political leadership in Wuhan.

The duty to report fully and rapidly is the one key lesson China failed to learn from the SARS epidemic (Mackenzie, 2020: 78). However, Dr. Osterholm notes that the world had all the information it needed to fight the pandemic by January 20–24, including extraordinary details on the epidemiology of COVID-19, the genetic sequence, and the complete quarantine measures taken by China from January 23. He remarks: "In terms of spread of virus, the virus will do what it's got to do. There is very little we can do to stop or affect its spread."[22] He also predicted the full pandemic on January 20, urging the world

---

[20] Source: Susan Lawrence. May 11, 2020. "COVID-19 and China: A Chronology of Events (December 2019–January 2020)." Congress Research Services Report # R46354. Available from: https://crsreports.congress.gov/product/pdf/r/r46354.

[21] Source: Remarks by Dr. Zhong Nan Shan at the online event hosted by Harvard Medical School and MassCPR as part of Worldwide Week at Harvard on October 7, 2020, and titled "Global Perspectives on COVID-19."

[22] Source: Containing COVID-19: Top Epidemiologist Dr. Michael Osterholm from Intelligence Matters on Apple Podcasts. https://podcasts.apple.com/ca/podcast/intelligence-matters /id1286906615?i=1000474413390.

to fully mobilize. That, however, did not happen in many countries, and weeks were wasted.

Throughout this period and especially after January 20, it remains crucial to acknowledge the extraordinary work and sacrifice of Chinese doctors and healthcare workers, as well as of China's people generally (Horton, 2020: 22). During Wuhan's 77-day lockdown, the population endured great hardship, while provinces around China sent medical teams and food supplies. By February, most major cities in China also enforced strict lockdown and mandatory testing across the country. Wuhan ended up building sixteen new makeshift hospitals with a capacity of 13,000 beds within nineteen days.[23] The virus was basically suppressed in China by March. "Between March 1 and October 5, there were only sporadic events in Heilongjiang, Jilin, Xinjiang, Beijing, including 2,921 import cases."[24] The turnaround in Wuhan after January 23 was extraordinary and was later acknowledged by the WHO as having given time to the world and saved countless lives. China pioneered key methods for fighting pandemics. Future research will better shed light on the sequence of events in December–January in Wuhan and what could have been done better, even under a state of uncertainty.

However, two more partial failures in global health governance took place outside China. One key issue relates to the architecture of global health governance and our failure of global preparedness for pandemics.

The keystone institution is the World Health Organization, based in Geneva, with its 194 member states. As a creature of the Westphalian state system, the WHO can only do what its powerful member states can agree to. It depends on access granted by sovereign states to do its work, a particular problem when it comes to China in 2003 (SARS) or in 2020 (COVID-19). Its budget is paltry, given the tasks of maintaining global health: less than $3 billion per year.[25] Over 80% of its funding is voluntary, and over 50% of the budget comes from foundations, private companies, and other nonstate actors.[26] This has the effect of pulling the WHO into various donor priorities, without the ability to concentrate on core capacities. Bill Gates long warned that the WHO was underfunded:

---

[23] Source: Remarks by Dr. Zhong Nan Shan at the online event hosted by Harvard Medical School and MassCPR as part of Worldwide Week at Harvard on October 7, 2020, and titled "Global Perspectives on COVID-19." For details on the sixteen temporary hospitals (and nineteen other planned ones), see Xinhuanet. www.xinhuanet.com/english/2020-03/12/c_138871374.htm (last accessed February 8, 2021).

[24] Source: ibid.

[25] $5.84 billion biennium budget for 2020 and 2021. Source: WHO. www.who.int/about/account ability/budget/.

[26] Source: Michael Peel, Anna Gross, and Clive Cookson. "WHO struggles to prove itself in the face of COVID-19." *Financial Times*. July 11, 2020. www.ft.com/content/c2809c99-594f-4649-968a-0560966c11e0?segmentId=b0d7e653-3467-12ab-c0f0-77e4424cdb4c.

"How many planes does it have; how many vaccine factories? We shouldn't think it's going to do things it was never intended to do" (Osterholm and Olshaker, 2017: 312). Osterholm and Olshaker argue that we cannot tackle pandemics without an integrated One Health approach (combining animal health and human health) and NATO-like rapid-reaction teams that can be quickly dispatched to new disease hot spots. We are fragmented and poorly equipped to face a sudden virus emergency.

In the case of COVID-19, the WHO took until January 30 to use its most important power, the power to declare a Public Health Emergency of International Concern (PHEIC). This was two days after its director general, Dr. Tedros Adhanom Ghebreyesus, visited Beijing. This was better than during SARS but probably ten days too late. It reflected an initial lack of consensus within its Emergency Committee, when it initially met on January 22–23 (Horton, 2020). It was deeply divided at that point. The less important but symbolic announcement of a global pandemic only came on March 11, also way too late.

The third failure has been a failure of reactivity by policymakers outside East Asia after January 20. The great loss of time for emergency preparedness between January 20 and early March in most of Europe and North America contributed to the health crisis that overwhelmed health-care systems. Horton writes: "Collectively, the deficiencies in decision-making reflect not only the surprising fragility of modern science-based societies, but also something far worse – inherent failures in the mechanics of Western democracies that threaten their very existence" (40).

The Global Economic Shock: Sudden Cardiac Arrest

The onset of the COVID-19 pandemic overwhelmed our interconnected globalization. In fact, Goh and Prantl argue: "COVID-19 is a system tipping-point – it will reset globalisation as we know it. Like the [Global Financial Crisis], this pandemic demonstrates that the costs of connectivity can outweigh its benefits. The fundamental challenge today is the trade-off between connectivity and resilience, the latter being a society's ability to bounce back from systemic shock" (Goh and Prantl, 2020).

In March 2020 (January–February for China), countries around the world shut down a large portion of their economic activity, as a by-product of lockdowns and "shelter in place" restrictions. Olivier Blanchard, the former chief economist of the IMF, puts it this way: "It is completely unprecedented. Overnight, we forced a decrease of production of 35%. No previous case in history with that speed and magnitude. Nothing happening within a few weeks at that level."[27] For example, the US GDP plunged by 32% in the second quarter of 2020, a historic drop, followed by a bounce back of similar size in the third quarter.[28] In early 2020, the IMF estimated that world growth for the year would reach 3.2%. By the end of 2020, the outcome was −3.3% instead, a drop of 6.5% from the trendline.[29] For some countries and regions, the losses of 2020 were even greater: −11.0% in Spain, −9.9% in the United Kingdom, −8.2% in Mexico, −8% in India, −7% in Latin America as a whole, −6.6% in the Euro area, −5.4% in Canada, −4.8% in Japan, and −3.5% in the United States.[30] As of October 2020, the IMF predicted a total output loss for the world of $11 trillion in 2020–21 and $28 trillion in 2020–25. These are enormous numbers, even if things improved to some degree in late 2020 and early 2021.[31]

Also crucial is the impact in terms of relative global economic power. Over 2020–21, China was estimated to grow by a cumulated 10.7%, while the United States was set to grow only a net 2.9% over the same two years. This positive number for the USA incorporates the great bounce back caused by vaccines and the Biden stimulus of 2021: it is 3 points higher than estimates in Fall 2020. The net outcome will be a likely increase in the ratio of China's GDP to the US GDP from 65% to about 72–75%, depending on inflation rates and exchange rate adjustments. This is likely to amount to a significant displacement. Indeed, in December 2020, the Japan Center for Economic Research (JCER) issued a report predicting that China's GDP would pass that of the United States in 2029 (normal scenario) or 2028 (in case of increased trade war), about five years ahead of forecasts made prior to the pandemic.[32] The report adds: "China is set to become a high-income country even earlier, in 2023, and its income per capita should reach $28,000 in 2035 – comparable to Taiwan's figure today." This may of course underestimate some key downside risks.

Within Southeast Asia, the COVID shock also has had differential impact: Vietnam, Indonesia, and Malaysia are all expected to end up 2020–21 with net

---

[27] Source: "Economist Olivier Blanchard on Global Economic Effects of COVID-19" from Intelligence Matters on Apple Podcasts. May 2020. https://podcasts.apple.com/ca/podcast/intelligence-matters/id1286906615?i=1000473009680.

[28] Source: https://tradingeconomics.com/united-states/gdp-growth.

[29] Source: IMF. October World Economic Outlook. April 2021. Available from https://www.imf.org/en/Publications/WEO/Issues/2021/03/23/world-economic-outlook-april-2021. Last accessed on May 4, 2021. Also detailed in Gita Gopinath's blog at https://blogs.imf.org/2020/10/13/a-long-uneven-and-uncertain-ascent/.

[30] Source: IMF. World Economic Outlook. April 2021.

[31] Source: Gita Gopinath's blog at https://blogs.imf.org/2020/10/13/a-long-uneven-and-uncertain-ascent/.

[32] Source: Japan Center for Economic Research. December 2020. "Asia in the coronavirus disaster: Which countries are emerging?" www.jcer.or.jp/english/asia-in-the-coronavirus-disaster-which-countries-are-emerging (last accessed January 23, 2021).

positive growth overall, while the economies of Singapore, the Philippines, and Thailand will likely end 2021 still smaller than their size at the end of 2019.[33]

Global trade decreased by about 8.5% in 2020.[34] It is expected to bounce back by 8.4% in 2021. That means that global trade will have experienced net stagnation over the combined 2020–21 period. However, trade in Asia will decline by about 4.5% only.[35]

One positive impact of this global economic shock was a large overall drop of CO_2 emissions by about 9%, or 1.6 gigatons, for the first half of 2020, the largest decrease since 1900 (Liu et al., 2020). For the full year 2020, however, global CO2 emissions dropped by only 4%.[36] The effect is particularly large in the United States, Europe, and India. But it is a one-time short-term drop that may not make a fundamental difference in the long-term battle against climate change.

Implication of the Economic Shock: A Great Social Shock

A social shock of enormous proportions has been induced across the world by the economic crisis. The COVID-19 shock has thrown in reverse a three-decade process of economic empowerment and poverty reduction around the world. As well, it has generated great inequality within societies. The United Nations Development Project (UNDP) evaluates that 2020 will see the first regression in the human development index since 1990, dwarfing the impact of the 2008 Global Financial Crisis.[37] In fact, the magnitude of the loss is such that it erases the gains of several years at once.

Inequality was already becoming politically explosive prior to COVID-19, as seen in countries such as the United States, France, and China. Globalization without strong policy corrections rewards cities and some economic sectors more than rural areas and associated industries. COVID-19 deepened this problem by delivering a double whammy. First, it hit service and blue-collar workers more directly by shutting down their sector of activity, while technology or professional services continued to thrive. Second, it accelerated the trend of digitalization and reinforced the digital divide between global winners such as Amazon and local losers such as traditional shops. Big tech companies

---

[33] Source: *Nikkei Asia*. December 29, 2020. "Vietnam, Indonesia and Malaysia seen fully recovering in 2021." https://asia.nikkei.com/Economy/Vietnam-Indonesia-and-Malaysia-seen-fully-recovering-in-2021 (last accessed January 23, 2021).

[34] Source: IMF. World Economic Outlook. April 2020.

[35] Source: WTO. October 2020. www.wto.org/english/news_e/pres20_e/pr862_e.htm.

[36] Source: IMF. April 2021. World Economic Outlook, p. 21.

[37] UNDP. October 2020. *COVID-19 and Human Development: Assessing the Crisis, Envisioning the Recovery*. Available from http://hdr.undp.org/sites/default/files/covid-19_and_human_development_0.pdf, p. 6.

experienced enormous gains in the stock market. Zakaria argues that dealing with such divisive inequality and related anger will be one of the greatest challenges in the post-pandemic world (Zakaria, 2020).

At the aggregate level, COVID-19 has generated a huge gap between countries that can spend their way out of the crisis and print money through their central banks and countries that simply cannot. This gap has induced a great financing need that the global governance architecture must address. Eichengreen writes: "This time, low-income countries are at risk of a crisis that will dwarf anything in the advanced-country world. Addressing their plight should be priority number one on humanitarian grounds, but also because what happens there will spill back onto the rest of the world through both economic and epidemiological channels" (Eichengreen, 2020).

The World Bank estimates that COVID-19 "may push an additional 88 million to 115 million people into extreme poverty this year, with the total rising to as many as 150 million by 2021, depending on the severity of the economic contraction."[38] World Bank President David Malpass also warned that up to 1.4% of the world population could be pushed back into poverty. This is the greatest increase in poverty in decades.

The shocks on human populations have come instantly through various parallel channels: rapid capital outflows from developing and emerging countries, collapsing commodity prices, and falling remittances from migrants to their families. The digital divide has accentuated the social cost, given that many workers were unable to have stable Internet access and work from home. In November 2020, the managing director of the IMF, Kristalina Georgieva, declared:

> I am very concerned because IMF research shows very clearly that every single pandemic that we have experienced over the last years from SARS to H1N1 to Zika, they all led to increase in inequality that was sustained years after the pandemic was over. And we are risking to see the same on a much larger scale because of COVID-19. And actually, early data already ringed the alarm bell in that regard. We also have a very unique situation with this crisis, with regard to education. We are seeing, massively, children dropping out of school and girls less likely to return in the future. We're also seeing kids that do not have access to the Internet, basically losing a long time that translates into loss of their ability to be productive in the future. I'm also worried about the impact of the crisis ... on gender inequality. Already, women are paying a higher price.[39]

---

[38] World Bank. October 7, 2020. Press Release. www.worldbank.org/en/news/press-release/2020/10/07/covid-19-to-add-as-many-as-150-million-extreme-poor-by-2021.

[39] Source: Transcript of IMF podcast: Kristalina Georgieva Talks Inequality with Oxfam. November 27, 2020. https://content.govdelivery.com/accounts/USIMF/bulletins/2ad5419.

UN Women has indeed documented how COVID-19 had erased years of efforts to count women's work and spread the home chore burden. With COVID-19, data shows a huge regression in this trajectory.[40] In the words of UN Women Deputy Executive Director Anita Bhatia, "everything we worked for, that has taken 25 years, could be lost in a year."[41]

The impact on school-aged children around the world also has been devastating. According to the World Bank, at least 72 million more children have been pushed into "learning poverty" in 2020, meaning that they won't be able to read and write by age ten.[42]

The Failure of Global Governance in Response to COVID-19 Shocks

Unlike in 2008–9, the global system did not work, and great powers failed to cooperate and face the crisis together. This was due to a combination of contextual factors prior to COVID-19 and decisions and strategic interactions of leaders during the COVID-19 pandemic.

To be sure, the global context was not propitious for effective cooperation. Prior to the irruption of the pandemic, the international system had just experienced a historic shift in the global balance of power that saw 21% of global GDP shift hands from developed to emerging (non-Western) countries in just eighteen years (Tiberghien, 2020). Such historic shifts are sources of great friction. Additionally, the world went through several years of conflict over multilateral institutions. Furthermore, key global institutions created right after World War II are in urgent need of reform and modernization. The inequalities and displacements caused by globalization in many Western countries led to the rise of populist movements focused on national issues. The legacy of the Global Financial Crisis of 2008–9 continued to generate anger, frustrations, and political ripple effects (Tooze, 2018). Global trade peaked in the wake of the GFC, ushering a period of "slowbalization" (Irwin, 2020). Adding to those stresses, climate change and the fourth industrial revolution, anchored in digitalization and artificial intelligence, generated more uncertainty and social divisions. Politically, the years leading up to COVID-19 witnessed hardening regimes in China and Russia and an insurgent America led by Donald Trump that chose to turn against the Liberal International Order it created (Kagan, 2018; Ikenberry, 2018).

---

[40] Source: UN Women. November 25, 2020. "Whose time to care: Unpaid care and domestic work during COVID-19." Brief. https://data.unwomen.org/publications/whose-time-care-unpaid-care-and-domestic-work-during-covid-19 (accessed November 27, 2020).

[41] Source. BBC. www.bbc.com/news/world-55016842.

[42] Source: World Bank. December 2, 2020. www.worldbank.org/en/news/press-release/2020/12/02/pandemic-threatens-to-push-72-million-more-children-into-learning-poverty-world-bank-outlines-new-vision-to-ensure-that-every-child-learns-everywhere (last accessed January 23, 2021).

This was not an auspicious environment for global cooperation. In a way, SARS-COV-2 proved to be a truly nasty virus: it chose one of the worse moments to rear its head in our world.

The big point about global governance reactivity in 2020 is this: high-level management mechanisms at the global level have mostly failed, including the UN Security Council, the G7, the G20, and what used to be bilateral dialogue between the two core powers, the US–China Strategic & Economic Dialogue. This failure crippled the ability of the world community to answer the crisis effectively through coordinated global health measures and travel control, cooperation on WHO capacity, trade stabilization, or a rapid increase in financial resources of the IMF. Even the race to find and purchase vaccines was launched on a competitive national basis, without initial global coordination.[43] This collective failure has two main roots: the Trump administration's opposition to multilateralism (as encapsulated in its slogan of America First) and the accelerating USA–China rivalry. It meant that the global system would not function at the capacity and speed required. Instead, it would have to rely on second-tier institutions, more informal networks, and regional coordination.

In the end, not all was lost. Below the leadership level, global institutions worked hard to generate some innovations. Even after the United States pulled out of the WHO entirely on May 29 to unanimous global outrage, the WHO soldiered on and did its best to share information about COVID-19, launch an inquiry into the virus's origins, and play a leading role in accelerating vaccine research and diffusion around the world. The WHO partnered with the European Union and global foundations to launch a new multi-stakeholder platform, the Act-Accelerator, defined in these words: "Launched at the end of April 2020, at an event co-hosted by the Director-General of the World Health Organization, the President of France, the President of the European Commission, and The Bill & Melinda Gates Foundation, the ACT-Accelerator brings together governments, health organizations, scientists, businesses, civil society, and philanthropists who have joined forces to speed up an end to the pandemic."[44] This coalition received a further boost at the Paris Peace Forum in November 2020 with new pledges of $500 million from France, the European Union, Spain, the Gates Foundation, and others.[45]

---

[43] Sources on vaccine hoarding: *The Economist*. November 12, 2020. www.economist.com /graphic-detail/2020/11/12/rich-countries-grab-half-of-projected-covid-19-vaccine-supply and Duke Global Health Innovation Center. 2020. Launch and Scale Speedometer. Duke University. Retrieved from: https://launchandscalefaster.org/covid-19.

[44] Source: WHO. www.who.int/news/item/26-06-2020-act-accelerator-update.

[45] Source: Paris Peace Forum. https://parispeaceforum.org/2020/11/25/3-days-to-bounce-back-to -a-better-planet-reviewing-the-success-of-the-third-edition/.

Under the Act-Accelerator's umbrella, the COVAX vaccine alliance also developed. It is another multi-stakeholder partnership. Officially, "COVAX is co-led by Gavi, the Coalition for Epidemic Preparedness Innovations (CEPI) and WHO. Its aim is to accelerate the development and manufacture of COVID-19 vaccines, and to guarantee fair and equitable access for every country in the world."[46] Ngozi Okonjo-Iweala, then board chair of Gavia and WHO special envoy on global collaboration to fight COVID-19, explained that the COVAX coalition launched more smoothly than expected in Fall 2020, as most countries joined, including EU countries, Japan, Canada, China, India, Korea, and ASEAN countries.[47] Only the United States and Russia stayed out in 2020. But President Biden turned things around and took the United States into COVAX through an executive order on the first day of his presidency on January 20, 2021.

The goal of COVAX is to reduce individual vaccine risks by pooling a large number of vaccine purchases from twelve manufacturers, while ensuring that developed countries pay for the poorer countries. The target of COVAX is to obtain 2 billion doses of vaccines in 2021 and to provide half of those to developing countries free of charge. In Okonjo-Iweala's words, with the Act-Accelerator, "we want to make sure that no country is standing in the queue, while bigger richer countries are taking the vaccine." The vaccine "must be treated as global public good. I cannot grab all vaccines in my country." And she adds: "Interconnectedness will bring back the disease to countries that feel safe. We must make it available for all. We must have equitable allocation."[48] The November 2020 G20 meeting endorsed both the Act-Accelerator and COVAX.

On the financial side, the global economy was kept afloat through two engines: national stimulus packages of developed economies plus China that reached a total of about $11.5 trillion in 2020;[49] and massive purchases of bonds by large central banks in developed economies. The Fed also extended dollar liquidities to middle-income US allies in various parts of the world. These actions prevented a systemic collapse but generated an increase of debt of about 20% of GDP in 2020 in advanced economies alone.[50]

---

[46] Source: WHO. www.who.int/initiatives/act-accelerator/covax.

[47] Source: GAVI. www.gavi.org/news/media-room/172-countries-multiple-candidate-vaccines-engaged-covid-19-vaccine-global-access.

[48] Source: live online remarks at the *Foreign Affairs* September/October 2020 issue launch event: What Happens When We Have the Vaccine? September 8, 2020.

[49] Source: IMF. Surveillance note. November 2020. www.imf.org/external/np/g20/pdf/2020/111920.pdf.

[50] Source: IMF. World Economic Outlook Database. April 2021. www.imf.org/en/Publications/WEO/weo-database/2021/April (last accessed May 4, 2021).

The system did not perform as well with respect to emerging and developing economies, which also faced massive fiscal needs in order to alleviate job losses and economic regression. One proposal on the table at the G20 on April 15, 2020, suggested letting the IMF issue between $500 billion and $1 trillion of its own currency, the Special Drawing Rights (SDR), similar to actions of 2008, when $250 billion was issued. This influx would be allocated according to the quotas of various countries; but leaders such as Ed Truman, Gordon Brown, and Larry Summers advocated for developed countries to share their quotas with developing countries (Nye, 2020). In the end, the United States vetoed the proposal at the G20, officially because too little money would go to developing countries but also because it would end up supporting countries like Iran and Venezuela. Furthermore, issuances of SDRs have often been linked to discussions of voting rights in the IMF, an issue that China is eager to push given its current 6.2% voting share, compared to a size of at least 16% of the world economy. The United States was eager to avoid that conversation.

Instead, the G20 approved a proposal prepared by the IMF and the World Bank to suspend debt service payments for the poorest countries in 2020. This became the Debt Service Suspension Initiative (DSSI), which was extended to June 2021 at the November G20. By November 2020, the DSSI had only helped forty-six countries (out of seventy-three eligible ones) for a total of $5.7 billion (including $1.9 billion from China).[51] The DSSI has brought increased cooperation between China and the Club of Paris creditors, itself a significant development.

On the trade side, the response was marked by confusion and rivalry. On December 11, 2019, the Appellate Body of the WTO – the peak component of the Dispute Settlement Mechanism – ceased functioning, with the United States having vetoed the nomination of new judges since 2017. So, 2020 was the first year since 1995 without a functioning global dispute settlement process in trade. In the midst of the pandemic, on May 14, the director general of the WTO, Roberto Azevêdo, abruptly resigned after expressing frustrations with the inability of the United States, the European Union, China, and Japan to coordinate their response to the COVID-19 pandemic.[52] The result was a vacuum at the top of this crucial organization in the midst of a global crisis. An intense race ensued with eight candidates for the job. On October 28, representatives from

---

[51] Source: Riyad G20 Communique. November 2020. www.g20.utoronto.ca/2020/2020-g20-leaders-declaration-1121.html. Regarding China's role, see Ye Yu in *East Asia Forum*. October 7, 2020. www.eastasiaforum.org/2020/10/07/how-to-assess-chinas-participation-in-the-g20-debt-service-suspension-initiative/.

[52] Source: *New York Times*. May 14, 2020, www.nytimes.com/2020/05/14/business/wto-chief-roberto-azevedo.html.

the 164 members of the WTO met and reached an overwhelming majority in favor of Dr. Ngozi Okonjo-Iweala, the former finance minister of Nigeria and leader of GAVI. That included support from the European Union, Japan, and China. The United States vetoed the appointment, however, adding to the sense of crisis in the global trading system.[53] In turn, the US proposal to have the American Alan Wolff serve as acting director general in the short term was vetoed by China, leading to the absence of even an interim leader.[54] On February 5, Biden broke the deadlock and approved Dr. Okonjo-Iweala as DG.

A modicum of stabilization in terms of dispute settlement came with the creation of the multi-party interim appeal arbitration arrangement (MPIA) pursuant to Article 25 of the WTO, at the initiative of the European Union and Canada on March 27. The group included the European Union and fifteen other WTO members (Australia, Brazil, Canada, China, Chile, Colombia, Costa Rica, Guatemala, Hong Kong, Mexico, New Zealand, Norway, Singapore, Switzerland, and Uruguay).[55] On April 15, the EU noted that Taiwan (Chinese Taipei) was also involved in the negotiations,[56] but it was not among the final signatories.

Japan had been part of the two-year-long discussions in the smaller Ottawa group of thirteen WTO members (excluding the United States and China) convened by Canada to find a solution to the WTO crisis.[57] However, in 2020, Japan chose not to join the MPIA, preferring to put the priority on negotiating with the United States over the Appellate Body itself. China, by contrast, had not been part of the Ottawa group but joined the MPIA in the end. South Korea, a member of the Ottawa Group, had joined the initial declaration at the Davos Forum on January 24, 2020, of the EU+16 group, but it did not sign the agreement in March. Within ASEAN, only Singapore is a member. India is not a party to the MPIA. By April 30, when the WTO issued a formal notification on the MPIA, the group had grown by three more members: Hong Kong, Iceland, and Pakistan.[58] On July 31, four more countries joined: Benin,

---

[53] Source: *The Guardian*. October 28, 2020. www.theguardian.com/world/2020/oct/28/us-blocking-selection-of-ngozi-okonjo-iweala-to-be-next-head-of-wto.

[54] Source: *Financial Times*. October 28, 2020. www.ft.com/content/94794d23-00c4-43df-a09f-a7c1d51d94ce.

[55] Source: Trade and ISDS news. August 2, 2020. https://tradeisds.com/wto-members-establish-mpia/.

[56] Source: European Council. April 15, 2020. www.consilium.europa.eu/en/press/press-releases/2020/04/15/council-approves-a-multi-party-interim-appeal-arbitration-arrangement-to-solve-trade-disputes/.

[57] Source: Canadian government. www.canada.ca/en/global-affairs/news/2019/05/ottawa-group-and-wto-reform.html (last accessed February 8, 2021).

[58] Source: WTO. April 30, 2020. https://tradeisds.com/wp-content/uploads/2020/05/1A12.pdf.

Ecuador, Montenegro, and Nicaragua. Then, arbitrators from ten MPIA members were nominated.[59] The MPIA is a valuable effort to maintain multilateral dispute resolution, but it is hobbled by the absence of key trading nations such as Japan, Korea, India, and of course the United States. By Spring 2021, it became clear that there was no rapid way out of the crisis of the Appellate Body, as the Biden team concurred with some of the deep grievances expressed by the Trump administration against the quasi-judicial functions taken on by the body over the years.

The case of the MPIA illustrates another key dimension of global governance during the COVID-19 crisis. While global high-level coordination mostly failed due to disagreements among leading powers, there was significant innovation at the cross-regional or "minilateral" level (agreements among a small number of willing countries and parties) and at the regional level. The COVID-19 environment broke diplomatic obstacles among like-minded countries and allowed for an unprecedented increase in direct contacts among foreign ministries at the highest levels. One such example is the Ministerial Coordination Group on COVID-19 (MCGC) led by Canada, along with Brazil, France, Germany, Indonesia, Italy, Mexico, Morocco, Peru, the Republic of Korea, Singapore, Turkey, and the United Kingdom, to support global transport and multilateralism during COVID-19. On April 17, they issued a joint declaration, in which signatory countries committed themselves to maintaining critical global supply links.[60]

Another example is the Coronavirus Global Response Initiative launched on April 24 as an international online pledging event cohosted by Canada, the European Union, France, Germany, Spain, Norway, the United Kingdom, Japan, Saudi Arabia, and Italy, with the aim of accelerating global scientific cooperation and raising funds for health solutions to COVID-19. By November 2020, this coalition has raised €15.9 billion.[61]

Additionally, France and Germany co-led the creation of the 48-country Alliance for Multilateralism (including Canada, Japan, Korea, and Singapore), which met on the margins of the UN General Assembly in September 2020 to reaffirm its commitment to multilateral solutions in climate, health, digital technology, and gender equality.[62]

---

[59] Source: Trade and ISDS news. August 2, 2020. https://tradeisds.com/wto-members-establish-mpia/.

[60] Source: Global Affairs Canada. April 17, 2020. www.canada.ca/en/global-affairs/news/2020/04/declaration-of-the-ministerial-coordination-group-on-covid19covid19-on-maintaining-essential-global-links.html.

[61] Source: https://global-response.europa.eu/index_en.

[62] Source: https://multilateralism.org/agenda/#update-covid19-ministerial-video-conference.

In terms of cooperation at the regional level, Asia made key advances, as Sections 4 and 5 in particular explain. It should be noted that Africa and Europe also made significant progress. Dr. Salim Abdool Karim, director of the Centre for the AIDS Programme of Research in South Africa (CAPRISA) and member of the coronavirus task force of the Africa Centres for Disease Control and Prevention, noted recently that the four-year-old and continent-wide African CDC succeeded in generating an unprecedented coordinated response across the continent.[63] This response included the creation of an early COVID-19 task force, a joint platform to coordinate purchases of PPE and combine purchasing power, a partnership to accelerate COVID-19 testing, and the creation of the African Union COVID-19 Fund. The African CDC encouraged leaders to make a commitment on wearing masks, and it paid off. Africa also benefited from its youth dividend and lower levels of international travel than other regions. At the time of writing, Africa actually stands out for having lower numbers of cases and deaths than one might have feared (except in South Africa), although this may reflect underreporting.

The European Union also made major progress during the pandemic after a very difficult and fractious start in February–April. Scenes of Chinese and Russian planes delivering PPE in Italy and other European countries contrasted with intra-European embargoes on the mutual sharing of such resources and galvanized Europeans to act. Europe's sense of solidarity and reputation for competence suffered greatly in the early months of the pandemic. However, the dynamic changed on May 18, when a Franco-German summit led to a commitment by both Angela Merkel and Emmanuel Macron to work toward creating a European bond program of up to €500 billion. Macron called this the most important breakthrough since the creation of the European Union. This was followed by an agreement by the twenty-seven European leaders at the EU Council Summit of July 17–21 (the longest summit in EU history) to create the Recovery and Resilience Facility (RRF). The €750 billion fund financed by European bonds managed by the European Commission (and involving non-Euro members as well) is a historic first for Germany and the EU. It is meant to cover up to €390 billion of direct recovery grants to countries hit badly by COVID-19, such as Italy and Spain, while focusing on long-term climate and digital investments.[64] The EU did face delays in the fall, as Poland and Hungary held the deal up for several months due to their opposition to the language on

---

[63] Source: Remarks by Dr. Salim Abdool Karim at the online event hosted by Harvard Medical School and MassCPR as part of Worldwide Week at Harvard on October 7, 2020, and titled "Global Perspectives on COVID-19."

[64] Source: EU Council. www.consilium.europa.eu/en/policies/eu-recovery-plan/.

"rule of law." A breakthrough finally came on December 10, and the deal was approved by the EU Council.

Table 1 summarizes the various actions taken at the global and regional levels by main issue areas with indicators of effectiveness (high, medium, and low).

In sum, the multilateral system proved ill prepared for the COVID-19 emergency, and established multilateral organizations became paralyzed by tensions between the United States and China and by the US opposition to global institutions. COVID-19 once again revealed the crucial position of the United States at the heart of the Liberal International Order and the need for mutual toleration among the two great powers if humanity is to deal with global challenges such as pandemics and the climate emergency. Ad hoc minilateral coalitions and regional coordination at the level below global organizations did spring into action and picked up some of the slack, albeit with limits. By the end of 2020, it was clear that the global response to support developing countries hurt by the COVID-19 shock was inadequate.[65] Going forward, leadership from the Biden administration (and China) are essential at the global level.

3 Institutional Capacity, Social Cohesion, and Successes at Home

The triple COVID-19 shock proved to be a real pressure cooker for domestic policymaking around the world. By generating concomitant health, socioeconomic, and geopolitical shocks, it tested the resilience and legitimacy of every government around the world. This is also the first geo-economic health crisis in the age of social media. Billions of people found themselves in lockdown with smartphones to express their frustrations and their version of events. This situation opens the door to demagogues and unscrupulous policy entrepreneurs.

Yet, in the face of such global disruptions and in contrast to the particularly high human cost paid by people in Europe, North America, and Latin America, Asian trajectories stand out. No Asian country (except Iran) suffered as high a mortality rate as countries in these three other regions.

I argue here that the broad East Asian formula involves high preparedness, good governance focused on science and bureaucratic competence, varying degrees of acceptance for measures that focus on collective security over individual freedom (given past historical narratives), and high-quality communication. There was also a relatively high degree of congruence in COVID-19 measures across the region, due to long-standing trends of norm diffusion over past decades that reinforced domestic institutions. The supply-side provision of

---

[65] Source: *Financial Times*. November 18, 2020. www.ft.com/content/f665b6d2-79f8-49e9-9c93-3602c42ecf83.

Table 1 Global governance performance in 2020 in response to COVID-19

	Low	Medium	High
Health	Slow reactivity Vaccine nationalism	• WHO + World Health Assembly agreement • Multilateral Ministerial Coordination Group on COVID-19 (MCGC)	• Act-Accelerator • COVAX vaccine alliance • Africa CDC joint purchase platform + AU COVID-19 Response Fund
Economic, financial, and social stabilization	G20: SDRs blocked, but DSSI approved	• IMF + World Bank and DSSI incubation • Finance in Common Summit (Paris) • EU Recovery and Resilience Facility (RRF) • AIIB–ADB work	Central bank coordination (Fed, ECB, BOJ, BOE …)
Trade and investment	WTO	• Ottawa Group • Multiparty Interim Appeal Arbitration Arrangement (EU+15)	• RCEP: Asia stabilization • EU–China Comprehensive Agreement on Investments (CAI)
Politics and security	• UN Security Council • G7 • No USA–China summit • China–India conflict		

science-based Weberian institutions is complemented by a high level of social cohesion and high expectations toward the state in times of crisis in most East Asian cases.

The Institutional Roots of East Asian Performance in Response to COVID-19

To be sure, there is a great variation in responses to COVID-19 throughout East Asia and over time. However, some common threads stand out as key take-aways. First, most (not all) East Asian nations had plans, laws, and structures ready to deal with pandemics at short notice, even when their health-care delivery system was limited. Second, the seventeen years since SARS in 2003 saw a reinforcement of preparedness and human capital. At the heart, these readiness plans relied on rapid reaction and central coordination capacity around a disease control center run by health professionals. In all East Asian countries, saving lives in the midst of a natural disaster is seen as the primary duty of the government.

The roots of these institutions are profound. Due to a combination of historical, cultural, and situational factors, most East Asian economies emerged from the pre-modern era with meritocratic bureaucracies and late-developing economic models relying on strong states alongside markets and entrepreneurs (Gerschenkron, 1962; Tiberghien, 2007; Wade, 1990). Japan experimented first with this model of mixed political economy in the wake of its Meiji Restoration in 1868 and achieved great economic success (Johnson, 1982). Japan also managed to revive and improve this model in the wake of the destruction of World War II, before playing a leading role in spreading this model and its success to East Asian "tiger" economies and Southeast Asia in a sequence characterized as the "flying geese" pattern (Akamatsu, 1962). Deng Xiaoping closely observed Japanese and East Asian (as well as European) successes before launching the Chinese reform and opening up process in 1978–9. Deng's historic ten-day trip to Japan in October 1978 was followed by a study mission that "outlined how China could learn about economic management from Japan" (Vogel, 2011: 308).

In his magisterial review of Asia's development over several centuries, Nayyar observes that most Asian countries share similar histories of "precipitous decline" (Nayyar, 2019: 28) from 1820 to the 1950s (with some exceptions, such as Japan and Singapore); structural transformation, industrialization, and economic and social progress after the 1960s; and "strategic integration with, rather than passive insertion into, the world economy" from the 1970s to the present (152). Crucially, he also argues that throughout the region "governments performed a critical role, ranging from leader to catalyst or supporter, in the economic transformation of Asia" (176). They all saw the state and the market as "complements." Nayyar notes that "China emulated these developmental states," albeit in a different political context (176). The experience of increased connectivity in recent years has been correlated with higher complementarities and increased growth (Khanna, 2019; Calder, 2019).[66]

In sum, East Asian countries such as China, Korea, or Indonesia (Java) share a common experience of economic collapse after centuries of prosperity and of revival through a mixed capitalist system that embedded a balance between market entrepreneurialism (World Bank, 1993) and a competent state as catalyst and coordinator (Okimoto, 1989). What is striking is that, for all the many economic reforms and struggles of the post-1990s, the core consensus around this equilibrium is embedded in dominant norms and narratives.

These similarities in governance and institutions transcend regime types. However, in the democratic pathway, we see more insistence on transparency, accountability, clear communication (Korea, Taiwan, New Zealand, Australia). Yet, Korea or Taiwan accepted higher constraints on privacy than North American or European democracies, including the public sharing of geolocation data on websites (without names) in the case of Korea.

The practical implication with respect to the pandemic is that East Asian countries focused on solving the health crisis and saving lives first. Alvelda, Ferguson, and Mallery studied the measures taken by the United States and contrasted those taken in East Asia. They conclude: "On the other hand, China, Taiwan, Australia, New Zealand, Iceland, and Singapore, Vietnam and Thailand, which all invested primarily in swift coronavirus suppression have effectively eliminated the virus and are seeing their economies begin to grow again. They are also in a positive feedback loop – in this case, a good one – where the reopening economies grow themselves without additional stimulus and suffer diminishing damage from the virus as cases dwindle" (Alvelda et al., 2020).

The specific success factors that emerge from the East Asian response are as follows:

1. Reliance on an advanced institutional capacity, including general health-care coverage (where present) as well as pre-existing legal capacity for

---

[66] See also the McKinsey Global Institute (MGI) discussion paper, "The future of Asia: Asian flows and networks are defining the next phase of globalization," September 18, 2019. Available from www.mckinsey.com/featured-insights/asia-pacific/the-future-of-asia-asian-flows-and-networks -are-defining-the-next-phase-of-globalization#.

pandemic emergencies (e.g., Korea, Taiwan, Singapore, Thailand; weaker in Japan).

2. Rapid creation of centralized government task forces (as early as January 2020 for many countries, as shown in Table 2) to coordinate testing capacity, quarantines and border controls, isolation measures, and socioeconomic measures. In Japan, a blueprint coordination plan was presented by the Cabinet on January 30 but only implemented on March 23, after passage of a new law.

3. Reliance on health scientists in key government positions (including, in Taiwan, the vice president), empowerment of national CDC, and lack of politicization of the pandemic response (except in Japan, where competition between the prime minister and the governor of Tokyo dominated the early months and simmered thereafter).

4. Use of quarantine, isolation measures, and varying degrees of rapid border controls (not in Korea, and late in Japan).

5. Rapid provision of tests and systematic use of testing in the population (except Japan, initially).

6. Reliance on universal mask-wearing. An INET comparative study concluded: "The single biggest and most consistent difference between the successful Asian countries and those Western countries that continue to struggle with COVID-19, is universal adoption of high-quality mask wearing and strict adherence to social distancing measures passed, *and enforced by*, national governments" (Alvelda et al., 2020).

7. Use of innovative contact-tracing apps, with various degree of individual consent, to triage individuals according to risk levels (China, Korea, Singapore, Taiwan, Vietnam).

8. Effective, precise, science-based, and empowering communication from leaders to citizens. This includes innovative and regular fireside-chat–style communication from Prime Minister Jacinda Ardern in New Zealand and Prime Minister Lee Hsien-Loong in Singapore, alongside more traditional science communication in many other countries.

In sum, we witness a broadly similar interpretation of the crisis through the lenses of collective health threat, good governance, and a science-based and nonpartisan response.

By and large, governments focused on pragmatic policies to fight COVID-19, seeing it as one new iteration in a series of pandemics (SARS, H1N1, MERS). There is also clearly a lot of information sharing, mutual observation, and mutual learning going on across East Asia, as government officials have been socialized to interact with each other in many summit meetings (ASEAN, ADB conferences, AIIB, APEC, etc.).

Table 2 Comparative factors driving East Asian COVID-19 performance in 2020 – selected cases

Cases	Health Capacity GHS Index	Central HQ/task force	Support for gov handling 11/26[67]	Decisions based on health science	Test per 1,000 04/1[68]	Support Location Quarantine 04/27[69]	Contact-tracing apps	Mask-wearing 05/01[70]
USA	High	No	36%	No	5.0	32%	No	63%
UK	High	No	35%	No	2.5	27%	No	13%
India	Low	No	76%	Partly	0.04	69%	Limited	81%
N.E.A.								
China	Low	1/25		Yes after 1/20	n/a		Yes	90%
Japan	High	3/23	42%	Partly	0.3	30%	Limited	84%
Korea	High	1/22		Yes	7.9		Yes	n/a
Mongolia	Low	1/19		Yes	n/a		No	n/a
Taiwan	n/a	1/20	82%	Yes	1.4	39%	Yes	87%
S.E.A.								
Indonesia	Med	3/13[71]	64%	Partly	0.03	53%	Yes	79%
Malaysia	High	2/11	76%	Yes	1.1	69%	Yes	86%
Myanmar	Low	3/13[72]		Yes	0.02		No	n/a
Philippines	Low	3/24[73]	63%	Mixed	0.2	73%	No	83%

Singapore	Med	1/22	87%	Yes	12.4	48%	Yes	90%
Thailand	High	3/27		Yes	1.0	63%	No	88%
Vietnam	Low	1/30	92%	Yes	0.9	81%	Yes	87%
Oceania								
Australia	High	2/27		Yes	11.6		Limited	25%
New Zealand	Med	1/28		Yes	6.0		Limited	

67 Source: YouGov COVID 19 Behavior Tracker. "Percentage of people who think the government is handling the issue of coronavirus very or somewhat well." Data points from November 26 (except Japan, for which May 4 is the last available point: https://yougov.co.uk/topics/international/articles-reports/2020/06/08/international-covid-19-tracker-update-8-june.

68 Source: Hannah Ritchie, Esteban Ortiz-Ospina, Diana Beltekian, Edouard Mathieu, Joe Hasell, Bobbie Macdonald, Charlie Giattino, and Max Roser. Oxford University. *Our World in Data.* Complete COVID-19 Dataset. https://ourworldindata.org/policy-responses-covid (retrieved November 29, 2020).

69 Source: https://yougov.co.uk/topics/international/articles-reports/2020/03/17/level-support-actions-governments-could-take.

70 Source: YouGov COVID-19 Behavior Tracker. "Percentage of people who say they are wearing a face mask when in public places." Data points on May 1 or within April 27–May 3 otherwise. https://yougov.co.uk/topics/international/articles-reports/2020/06/08/international-covid-19-tracker-update-8-june.

71 Source: *Jakarta Post.* www.thejakartapost.com/academia/2020/03/28/how-indonesia-is-expediting-its-response-to-covid-19.html (last accessed January 23, 2021).

72 Source: The Irrawaddy. www.irrawaddy.com/news/burma/myanmar-forms-civil-military-emergency-task-force-boost-covid-19-response.html (last accessed January 23, 2021).

73 Source: www.cnnphilippines.com/news/2020/3/24/Congress-Duterte-signature-special-powers-COVID-19.html (last accessed January 23, 2021).

It is also important to note that Japan has been leading a global effort toward universal health-care coverage at the G20 and the UN and played a key role in developing the health systems in Indonesia and Myanmar (Takuma, 2020), as well as in Vietnam.

Table 2 summarizes key traits of the East Asian response to COVID-19 in 2020. Everywhere, we observe a high degree of science-based decisionmaking. Three further features stand out: the early mobilization of centralized pandemic command centers; the very high and general adoption of masks; and the early and effective use of contact-tracking apps in a number of cases. Also striking is the high level of public support for the government's handling of the pandemic, as measured in November 2020, except for Japan. The rapid deployment of early testing (measured on April 1, 2020) only took place in Singapore, Australia, Korea, New Zealand, and Taiwan.

It is interesting to contrast those actions to the narrower list of measures tracked under the Oxford stringency index (Hale et al., 2020). The design team created a Government Stringency Index as a composite measure of nine response metrics. "The nine metrics used to calculate the Government Stringency Index are: school closures; workplace closures; cancellation of public events; restrictions on public gatherings; closures of public transport; stay-at-home requirements; public information campaigns; restrictions on internal movements; and international travel controls."[74] Looking at the overall metric on April 1, only Vietnam reached the maximum stringency, while Japan had among the lowest stringency values in the world. By contrast, many European countries, India, Central Asian countries, and others had reached maximum stringency. By September 10, most of Asia had lower stringency measures than South America, Africa, North America, and India.

In other words, the response in East Asia in 2020 has relied primarily on strategic rapid action and contact tracing, with the aim of avoiding long-term interruption of social life.

Social Cohesion and Social Trust

Discussing why Australia, China, Japan, and South Korea were able to perform better than Europe in introducing and sustaining detection, isolation, and tracing measures, the WHO's Mike Ryan noted that "higher levels of trust" in their governments enabled these governments to keep measures longer.[75] To be more

---

[74] Source: Our World in Data. Oxford. https://ourworldindata.org/covid-government-stringency-index.

[75] Source: *South China Morning Post.* October 20, 2020. www.scmp.com/news/world/europe/article/3106184/coronavirus-measures-europe-north-america-should-learn-asia-says (last accessed January 22, 2021).

precise, Ryan should have focused on the question of social trust within society, or the ability for people to trust others in their community and thus be ready to act for the public good. Stockwin observed that group solidarity and volunteering played a key role in the public support for strong COVID measures in East Asia. He notes that "communal values" in countries such as South Korea were a big part of the national success early in the pandemic (Stockwin, 2020). Goh and Prantl argue that COVID-19 demonstrates the importance of building social resilience to deal with increases in global connectivity (Goh and Prantl, 2020). When a crisis hits, society must pull together.

A full discussion of the concept of social cohesion and of the dense literature pertaining to it is beyond the scope of this Element. We focus here on the dimensions of horizontal trust among citizens within a society and the connection to a sense of common good. Recent years have seen a large effort to measure and quantify these dimensions, including through the huge endeavour of the World Values Survey.[76] We report here the findings from a couple of surveys taken in 2014 and 2020 for the purpose of an early plausibility test.

In 2014, Christian Larsen presented a paper at the United Nations on definitions and measurements of social cohesion. He emphasized the concept of "similarity of mind" and the importance of trust, especially horizontal trust. Using World Values Survey data from 2010–14, he found that the top twelve societies in terms of general social trust ("most people can be trusted") included China (ranked #2), New Zealand, Australia, Japan, and Singapore, as well as neighbours Kazakhstan and Kyrgyzstan. Taiwan and Korea were right behind the top twelve. Also in the top category were Northern European countries: Netherlands (#1), Sweden, and Estonia (Larsen, 2014: 8).

Ortiz-Ospina (2016) reports similar data on social trust using the results from the 2014 World Values Survey. A strong relation is shown overall between GDP per capita (PPP) and social trust. Predictably, we find a cluster of countries with both high GDP per capita and high social trust, including the Nordic countries and Netherlands at the top, followed by Australia, Switzerland, Germany, Canada, the US, Singapore, and Japan (all above 35% positive response to the question that most people can be trusted). However, the data also shows a cluster of outlying East Asian countries with very high social trust (between 35% and 60% positive), despite low GDP per capita: China, Vietnam, and Indonesia, followed by countries such as Kazakhstan, India, and Thailand.[77] China, with a GDP per capita in 2014 reported at just above $10,000, has a social trust level equivalent to that of the Netherlands and Sweden (GDP per

---

[76] Source: www.worldvaluessurvey.org/wvs.jsp (last accessed January 23, 2021).

[77] Source: Esteban Ortiz-Ospina. 2016. "Trust." https://ourworldindata.org/trust.

capita around $50,000). Vietnam, with an even lower GDP per capita, has a level equivalent to that of Switzerland.

These survey results taken years prior to the COVID-19 pandemic point to higher levels of social trust and belief in the common good in East Asia, Australia and New Zealand, and Northern Europe overall. In other words, it is not just that governments in East Asia had a plan and strong institutional capacity. It is also the fact that society accepted these measures for the sake of horizontal solidarity.

Individual Freedom versus Collective Responsibility

Pandemics, like other questions such as the climate emergency, raise profound questions about the balance between individual freedom and social responsibility. COVID-19 forced every society, every country, every community to take rapid yet profound decisions that involved a degree of compromise between saving lives in the community and maintaining individual freedom. Saving lives and the economic order required empowering the government to order limitations on some freedoms through lockdowns, quarantines, school and bar closures, and mask-wearing. Such compromises also require a degree of social agreement on the facts underlying the pandemic and a degree of trust in the various levels of government. These conditions have been deeply challenged in recent years in many countries.

This debate over facts and the role of government is connected to a debate over notions of individual freedom. In a recent philosophical essay, Jon Stewart has argued that the effort initiated by Hegel and others to free human nature from the burdens of tradition has shifted the notion of truth, culminating today "with a complete denial of any objective truth or validity." Individual rights seem to now include the right to assert a fictional reality against verifiable facts. He concludes: "For many people, this is a disturbing tendency in our modern world since it eliminates all sense of personal responsibility or culpability. Even the most heinous behaviour or action can always be justified with an appeal to the truth of the individual" (Stewart, 2020).

As shown in Table 2, COVID-19 has revealed that most East Asian societies support measures like general mask-wearing, quarantines, and even intrusive contact-tracing at the cost of privacy. Further analysis and survey work will be able to reveal if citizens consciously linked those measures to a sense of collective responsibility. The case studies in the rest of the chapter offer further analysis in particular national settings.

To be sure, there are also dangers in accepting limitations on freedom, especially through electronic surveillance. Yuval Harari calls our attention to the risk of "centralised monitoring and harsh punishments," urging all societies to find ways to implement competent measures by empowering citizens through clear communication and tools (Harari, 2020). Looking at Southeast Asia, Murray Hiebert warns: "Efforts to control the virus are giving authoritarian rulers the perfect cover to adopt draconian levers to rein in their opponents and critics" (Hiebert, 2020a). Finding a democratic pathway to deploy useful digital tools while protecting individual freedom and privacy will be a key agenda ahead for many societies around the world.

Measuring COVID-19 Performance

East Asia was at the epicenter of the COVID-19 pandemic. Countries such as Thailand, Japan, Korea, and Singapore have the most flight connections with Wuhan and other major cities in China. As expected, the first COVID-19 cases outside Wuhan were identified in Thailand (January 13), Japan (January 16), South Korea (January 20), Singapore (January 23), and Vietnam (January 23). Most of these cases preceded the first case identified in the United States (January 21 in Seattle). Yet all East Asian countries eventually managed to bring COVID-19 under control. Given that statistics about cases are highly uncertain and depend on the intensity of testing in each country, we can use the comparative number of fatalities per million inhabitants to compare national effectiveness in dealing with COVID-19. These numbers are more reliable but are still largely underreported in places like China, South Asia, Africa, and South America. Even then, the comparative proportions among regions and countries is a broadly valid measure of performance. Table 3 offers mortality data after one year (as of January 15, 2021) and groups countries into three categories: high, medium, and low. East Asian countries and Oceanian countries are highlighted in bold.

What stands out in Table 3? First, there are wide variations in outcomes around the world. Second, performance does not simply correlate with levels of development or regime types (democratic vs authoritarian). Third, East Asia and Oceania stand out as a broad region with the lowest deaths per capita across the region (ranging from less than 1 death per million in Taiwan, Vietnam, Thailand, and Mongolia to 93 in Indonesia). Fourth, South Asia has higher numbers, but they remain low to medium. By May 4, 2021, the picture changed quite a bit, with India's deaths per million reaching 163 and general recognition that the true number is much higher. Fifth, Africa also stands out with low numbers, though this likely reflects undercounting (especially in a case like Tanzania). Sixth, the United States and countries in Europe and Latin America (except Cuba and Uruguay) stand out with high mortality rates. The US (and

Table 3 Total COVID-19 mortality rate per million residents – selected cases ranked (as of February 6, 2021)[78]

HIGH (>700)		MEDIUM (61–699)		LOW (<60)	
(New Jersey, USA)	*2480*	Iran	695	**Myanmar**	**58**
(New York, USA)	*2300*	Ukraine	566	**Pakistan**	**54**
Slovenia	1737	Israel	586	**Bangladesh**	**50**
United Kingdom	1654	Canada	548	**Japan**	**50**
Italy	1505	Russia	514	Senegal	40
USA	1396	*(Ontario, Canada)*	449	**Australia**	**36**
Hungary	1348	Denmark	383	**South Korea**	**29**
(Texas, USA)	*1360*	Turkey	316	**Hong Kong**	**25**
Spain	1313	** **WORLD**	**296**	**Malaysia**	**26**
Mexico	1286	*(Hawaii, USA)*	290	Uzbekistan	19
Peru	1272	*(BC, Canada)*	247	Ethiopia	19
France	1209	Morocco	227	Cuba	21
Sweden	1200	Saudi Arabia	184	Tajikistan	9
(Quebec, Canada)	*1188*	Kazakhstan	166	Nigeria	8
(California, USA)	*1120*	Uruguay	139	**New Zealand**	**5.18**
Switzerland	1110	Finland	124	**Singapore**	**4.96**
Argentina	1087	**Indonesia**	**115**	**China**	**3.35**

Brazil	1082	India	**112**	Fiji	**2.23**
Poland	1030	Philippines	**101**	Thailand	**1.13**
Austria	888	Egypt	94	Papua New Guinea	**1.01**
Ecuador	850	UAE	92	Mongolia	**0.61**
Netherlands	844	Iceland	85	Taiwan	**0.38**
South Africa	779	Nepal	**70**	Vietnam	**0.36**
Germany	735	Algeria	66		

Note: East Asian, South Asian, and Oceanian cases are bolded for emphasis; provinces and US states are italicized. The table includes the two US states with the largest populations (California, Texas), the two states with the highest mortality (New York and New Jersey), as well as the state with the lowest mortality (Hawaii) to give a sense of the spread among US states. The three most populated provinces of Canada are also included. Numbers are certainly underreported in many countries. For example, body cremation counts in Wuhan at the start of the pandemic in early 2020 gave indications that deaths may be about three to ten times higher than reported. If that is correct, that would put the Chinese number at about 10 to 30 per million.

[78] Source: Hannah Ritchie, Esteban Ortiz-Ospina, Diana Beltekian, Edouard Mathieu, Joe Hasell, Bobbie Macdonald, Charlie Giattino, and Max Roser. Oxford Unversity. *Our World in Data.* Complete COVID-19 Dataset. https://ourworldindata.org/policy-responses-covid (retrieved February 7, 2021). Canadian provincial data as of February 7, 2021, from the Government of Canada. www.statista.com/statistics/110707 9/covid19-deaths-by-province-territory-canada/ (retrieved February 8, 2021). US state data as of February 8, 2021, from Johns Hopkins University. www.statista.com/statistics/1109011/coronavirus-covid19-death-rates-us-by-state/ (retrieved February 8, 2021). For Hong Kong, Worldometer data. www.worldometers.info/coronavirus/country/china-hong-kong-sar/ (retrieved February 7, 2021).

UK) situation started turning around after February 2021 with the rapid deployment of vaccines.

Just prior to the COVID-19 outbreak, three large private organizations – the Nuclear Threat Initiative (NTI), the Johns Hopkins Center for Health Security (JHU), and the Economist Intelligence Unit (EIU) – teamed up to develop the first-ever "comprehensive assessment and benchmarking of health security and related capabilities across the 195 countries."[79] They received funding from the Open Philanthropy Project, the Bill & Melinda Gates Foundation, and the Robertson Foundation. Their goal was to develop a systematic Global Health Security (GHS) Index to measure "national health security" capabilities in dealing with some of "the world's most omnipresent risks: infectious disease outbreaks that can lead to international epidemics and pandemics." The team systematically developed eighty-five sub-indicators grouped in six categories: prevention of pathogen emergence; early detection and reporting; rapid-response capacity; robust health systems; compliance with international norms; and overall risk environment. As luck had it, the international team produced the first Global Health Security Index report in October 2019.[80] They ranked all countries from 1 to 100 on each category and on an overall indicator. The report concluded that even some developed countries were ill-prepared for pandemics.[81]

Table 4 presents a selective ranking of countries by overall scores for pandemic preparedness as of late 2019. Focusing on larger developed, upper-income and middle-income developing countries, I identify three groups: high-capacity countries, medium-capacity countries, and low-capacity countries.

Table 4 includes a few surprising outcomes. Within Asia, Thailand and Korea are found to be the best-prepared countries, ahead of Japan and many developed countries. Malaysia also scores higher than Japan. China is ranked lower, along with Vietnam and the Philippines.

Table 5 compares actual mortality outcomes by category and the expected pandemic capacity measured by the GHS Index, identifying categories of

---

[79] Source: www.ghsindex.org/about/ (last accessed November 11, 2020).

[80] Source: Elizabeth Cameron, Jennifer Nuzzo, and Jessica Bell, co-leaders. October 2019. *Global Health Security Index: Building Collective Action and Accountability.* Nuclear Threat Initiative and Johns Hopkins University (with the support of the Economist Intelligence Unit). www .ghsindex.org/wp-content/uploads/2020/04/2019-Global-Health-Security-Index.pdf (last accessed November 29, 2020).

[81] Source: Johns Hopkins University Bloomberg School of Public Health. October 24, 2019. Global Health Security Index finds gaps in preparedness for epidemics and pandemics: Even high-income countries are found lacking and score only in the average range of preparedness. *ScienceDaily.* www.sciencedaily.com/releases/2019/10/191024115022.htm (retrieved November 11, 2020).

Table 4 Selected ranked Global Health Security Index scores by categories (October 2019)

High (60–84)		Medium (51–60)		Low (<=50)	
USA	84	Brazil	59	Ecuador	50
United Kingdom	78	**Singapore**	59	Mongolia	50
Netherlands	76	Argentina	59	Peru	49
Australia	76	Austria	59	**Vietnam**	49
Canada	75	Mexico	58	**China**	48
Thailand	73	**Indonesia**	57	**Philippines**	48
Sweden	72	Italy	56	Israel	47
Denmark	70	Poland	55	India	47
Korea	70	South Africa	55	Russia	44
France	68	Hungary	54	**Myanmar**	43
Switzerland	67	**New Zealand**	54	Uruguay	41
Germany	66	Turkey	52	Egypt	40
Spain	66			Cambodia	39
Malaysia	62			Senegal	38
Japan	60			Nigeria	38
				Iran	38
				Pakistan	36
				Cuba	35
				Nepal	35
				Bangladesh	35

overperforming and underperforming countries, relative to their measured capacities.

Several surprising findings appear in Table 5. First, the GHS Index proved to be a poor predictor of outcomes during COVID-19 for a large proportion of countries. Second, the United States, the United Kingdom, France, Spain, Switzerland, and Sweden stand out as countries that greatly underperformed relative to their objective health security capacity. Third, a few developed countries including Germany, Canada, and Austria mostly performed at the levels expected by their capacity (with signs of pandemic fatigue in Spring 2021). Fourth, all East Asian countries performed at least as well as, and often much better than, their expected capacity, whether much better (Vietnam, China, Myanmar), somewhat better (Singapore, New Zealand, Philippines), or just as expected (Thailand, Korea, Malaysia, Australia, Japan, Indonesia). Many African countries also stand out in terms of performance, although experts caution that more time will be needed to have robust and fully reliable data.

Table 5 COVID-19 performance of selected countries relative to pandemic capacity

COVID-19 death rate	GHS Index		
	High	**Medium**	**Low**
Low	Expected high performers	*Over-performers	** Super achievers
	Thailand	Singapore	Mongolia
	Korea	New Zealand	Vietnam
	Malaysia		China (post 1/23/20)
	Japan		Nigeria
	Australia		Cuba
			Ethiopia
			Senegal
			Uruguay
			Myanmar
			Pakistan
			Bangladesh
Medium	Under-performers	Expected medium performers	*Over-performers
	Germany	Turkey	Egypt
	Canada	Indonesia	Philippines
		Austria	India (until Spring 2021)
		South Africa	Russia
			Israel
High	** Super under-performers	Under-performers	Expected low performers
	Switzerland	Hungary	Iran
	Sweden	Brazil	Ecuador
	France	Mexico	Peru
	USA	Argentina	
	United Kingdom	Italy	
	Spain	Poland	

The data reveal the extent of the East Asian COVID-19 paradox: East Asian countries performed better than their objective pre-pandemic capacity would lead us to predict, and they show a high level of clustering among them.

In 2021, a new measure of success emerged: speed of vaccination for the population. One should note that this indicator is the result of a mix of factors, including degrees of innovation and corporate strength; priority access to supplies (by imposing export restrictions or paying higher prices or striking special contracts), and logistical efficiency. On that score measured as share of the population vaccinated with at least one dose on May 3, 2021, the leaders among major countries were Israel (60%), Chile (43%), the United Kingdom (52%), the United States (45%), Hungary (42%), Germany (29%), Canada (between 24% and 29%), the European Union (24%), and various Pacific islands.[82] The European Union stood at 3.7%. No Asian countries appeared in the top twenty-five, except Singapore (24%). China had managed to administer 280 million doses (about a quarter of worldwide doses administered), but this represented less than 20% of its population with at least one dose. These are early indicators of a potential second round against COVID-19 featuring the amazing speed of vaccine development in the United Kingdom and the United States. But East Asian countries have felt less of an urge to rush, given their greater control of the disease. Japan was the last G7 country to approve the COVID-19 vaccine. Minister of Administrative Reforms Kono Taro was put in charge of unfolding a rapid plan that saw him rise in popularity in February 2021. By April 29, 2021, Japan had administered only 3.5 million doses, and 2% of Japan's population had received at least one dose.

Measuring Economic and Social Performance in East Asia under COVID-19

As noted in Section 2, because they tackled COVID-19 more rapidly, East Asian economies as a whole are on track to suffer an economic shock that is less deep than that felt by the rest of the world. Table 6 presents summary estimates of the economic shock in the region.

Remarkably, several economies finished 2020 with a positive growth rate number: China, Vietnam, Myanmar, and Taiwan. They are also expected to bounce back rapidly in 2021 (except Myanmar, mired in the aftermath of the military coup). Other countries in the region have contained the shock but are suffering from loss of mobility, loss of tourism, and loss of commodity exports. The Philippines, Singapore, Thailand, and Australia are particularly hard hit. Also hit hard were Macao (−56% in 2020), due to the high dependence of its casino economy on tourism, and Hong Kong (−6.1% in 2020). On the whole, however, East Asian economies are emerging from the COVID-19 shock in a better position relative to the rest of the world. The same is true in terms of middle-class growth. According to Homi Kharas of the Brookings Institution,

---

[82] Source: *Financial Times* COVID-19 Vaccine Tracker (using Our World in Data from Oxford University). https://ig.ft.com/coronavirus-vaccine-tracker/?areas=gbr&areas=isr&areas=usa&areas=eue&cumulative=1&populationAdjusted=1 (last consulted May 4, 2021).

Table 6 Growth rate estimates for East Asian and Oceanian economies in 2020[83]

Regions	Growth rate in 2019	Est. 2020 GDP rate in April	2020 GDP final	2021 estimate
N. East Asia	**5.4**	**2.0**	**1.8**	**7.4**
China	6.1	2.3	2.3	8.1
Japan	0.3	−5.2	−4.8	3.3
Korea	2.0	1.3	−1.0	3.5
Mongolia	5.1	2.1	−5.3	4.8
Taiwan	2.7	1.8	3.1	4.6
S. East Asia	**4.4**	**1.0**	**−4.0**	**4.4**
Cambodia	7.1	2.3	−3.1	4.0
Indonesia	5.0	2.5	−2.1	4.5
Laos	5.0	3.5	−0.5	4.0
Malaysia	4.3	0.5	−5.6	6.0
Myanmar	6.8	4.2	+3.3	−9.8
Philippines	6.0	2.0	−9.6	4.5
Singapore	0.7	0.2	−5.4	6.0
Thailand	2.4	−4.8	−6.1	3.0
Vietnam	7.0	4.8	+2.9	6.7
Oceania				
Australia	1.9		−2.4	4.5
New Zealand	2.2		−3.0 *	4.0 *

"COVID-19 will probably reduce the speed of [global] middle class expansion by about one year. Almost all the growth will be in Asia because Asia seems to be dealing somewhat better than the rest of the world with COVID. Let me say that there is considerable uncertainty right now about South Asia (India, Pakistan, Bangladesh), and there is a downside scenario that is far worse, but assuming this does not come to pass, Asia will recover fast."[84]

---

[83] Source: Asian Development Bank. April 2021. *Asian Development Outlook Update*, www.adb.org/publications/asian-development-outlook-2021. For Australia, Japan, and New Zealand, the IMF's World Economic Outlook (April 2021) is used (p. 36).

[84] Personal email exchange with the author. June 15, 2020. See also www.brookings.edu/research/chinas-influence-on-the-global-middle-class/.

Battling COVID-19 on the Ground: Selected Cases from East Asia

China

China is the most dramatic case. As noted in Section 3, the pandemic surveillance process, early-warning mechanism, and rapid-response system partially failed in Wuhan between early December and January 20, in large part because of the focus of local authorities on their political priorities and fear of reporting bad news to Beijing. Once the team of Dr. Zhong Nan Shan came out publicly on January 20, China underwent a drastic turnaround and took extremely effective measures. Dr. Zhong explained how the most essential decision was the decision to fully control, rather than merely mitigate, the process of the virus, through strong quarantine and isolation measures to block transmission.[85] The measures were harsh – especially in Wuhan, cut off from the world for seventy-seven days after January 23. Initially, the lockdown created turmoil, with millions trying to escape the city between January 20 and January 23. There was an initial surge in patients seeking care and overwhelming the hospital capacity and a lack in initial support capacity given the absence of civil society. It took a couple of weeks for makeshift hospitals to be built, for outside resources to start pouring in, and for the state system to get into full gear.

Most cities followed Wuhan with their own lockdowns, enforced by local community party cells and police deployment. Measures included strict control of movement in and out of homes, along with temperature checks at the gates of all housing complexes. Only one household member was allowed to go shopping every two or three days after passing through ID, temperature, and mask checks (Li and Lu, 2020).

All schools in the country closed after January 20 (initially corresponding with the Chinese New Year break), and most stayed closed until mid to late April.[86] Afterward, partial closures took place in cities or provinces affected by small outbreaks, and holiday breaks were lengthened. From January 22 to September 20, gatherings of all sizes outside immediate family bubbles were restricted.

Jia Qingguo of Peking University has this assessment of the events in Wuhan and beyond: "The delay in taking more effective measures to address the epidemic turned out to be lethal. Soon the virus took over the city and spread beyond it. Then Beijing stepped in. It sacked Wuhan's leaders and took unprecedented measures to contain the virus, including locking down the city of

---

[85] Source: Remarks by Dr. Zhong Nan Shan at the online event hosted by Harvard Medical School and MassCPR as part of Worldwide Week at Harvard on October 7, 2020, and titled "Global Perspectives on COVID-19."

[86] Source: Random checks by the author with families in various provinces of China.

17 million, sending more than 40,000 medical staff and huge quantities of medical supplies, quickly building two large temporary hospitals and imposing the strictest social distancing policies in history nationwide. Except for essential industries and services, the country was shut down" (Jia, 2020).

The harsh lockdown led to a wave of online protests that partially overwhelmed controls in February, especially after the death of Dr. Li Wenliang, an early whistleblower and hero, from COVID-19 on February 7, at the age of only forty-five. During one month or so, China saw an outpouring of social media posts by tens of millions of people. In the words of Stanford's Zhou Xueguang, as resentment and criticism of government rose, an unprecedented "unorganized concerted effort in defiance of government censorship" took place around a report produced by Dr. Ai Fen.[87] She was the director of the emergency department at Wuhan Central Hospital and became one of the early whistleblowers on December 30 when she reported SARS-like patients. On March 10, she went public with her tale of how early findings were suppressed and was called the "Whistle-Giver" (发哨子的) by *Renwu* (People) magazine.[88] Her report was censored on the Internet. Yet within hours, and in a defeat for the AI-driven censorship system, web users posted versions in dozens of languages, including in pictures, reverse order, Q code, pinyin, Cantonese, ancient Chinese, oracle form, English, Italian, French, Japanese, Vietnamese, Hebrew, Morse code, music code, and others.

By April, however, the massive mobilization of the health and state infrastructure had succeeded in eradicating the virus. The dominant discourse on Chinese Internet shifted to the poor performance of Western systems in the battle with COVID-19. Singaporean historian Wang Gungwu puts the dramatic sequence of events that took place in China in January–March in a historical context. The Chinese people saw a great disaster, reminiscent of past black swans. This is often seen as a test of the ruler and his capacity to govern. He writes:

> What was striking was how quickly the anger of the people of Wuhan was replaced by acceptance and even gratitude for the official efforts to remedy the damage. This calls to mind how Chinese people in the past had reacted to official failures when dealing with disasters like epidemics, earthquakes or the massive Yellow and Yangzi river floods. Historical records were kept of everything that was thought to be unnatural and threatening to human lives. People affected by these disasters protested, which often led to violent

---

[87] Remarks by Dr. Zhou Xueguang. April 24, 2020. Panel titled "Social and Economic Impact of COVID-19 in Asia" at Stanford University's Freeman Spogli Institute.

[88] Source: *The Guardian*. March 11, 2020. www.theguardian.com/world/2020/mar/11/coronavirus-wuhan-doctor-ai-fen-speaks-out-against-authorities. Also: Wikipedia. https://en.wikipedia.org/wiki/Ai_Fen.

revolts. The mandarins and soothsayers would advise that the disasters were signs of Heaven's disapproval. The emperor would then try to introduce reforms to make the people's lives more bearable. If he failed to do that in time, he would be replaced or his dynasty would fall. (Wang, 2020)

In sum, the Chinese governance system was initially slow to react to the emerging COVID-19 crisis, and scientists were initially silenced by a local government bent on maintaining its large political events and keeping social order. Once the central government was fully mobilized on January 20, however, China unleashed unprecedented measures of testing, contact tracing, isolation, and rapid treatment that defeated the virus by the end of April. After initial anger at the suppression of information, the people cooperated with the tough measures, and the positive outcome has given way to a sense of achievement. Occasional outbreaks have appeared since May 2020, sometimes due to returning travellers and sometimes due to imported food. In each case, affected provinces (such as Hubei in December 2020) responded with massive lockdowns, systematic testing of entire cities, and contract tracing. China also remained closed to non-Chinese travellers throughout 2020 and the first half of 2021. But the measures have been effective.

Taiwan

Taiwan offers a remarkable case of success in tackling COVID-19 with a combination of effective governance and democratic accountability. Taiwan's vice president, Dr. Chen Chien-Jen, happens to be an epidemiologist with a doctorate from Johns Hopkins University. Reflecting upon what helped Taiwan weather the COVID-19 crisis, he highlights three key principles: prudent action (before the crisis); rapid response; and early deployment.[89] He adds that the stakes were higher for Taiwan, since Taiwan is not a WHO member and cannot count on rapid interactions with it. Additionally, this outbreak took place just after the Taiwanese presidential election on January 11 and just before the large-scale travel linked to Lunar New Year celebrations (starting January 25).

Taiwan's preparations for this crisis were heavily shaped by its SARS experience. Vice President Chen summarizes: "SARS revealed flaws, we rebuilt the system." This included an updated Communicable Disease Control Act (last revised in 2019), the preparation of medical supplies, and strong provisions for quarantine and against the dissemination of wrong information. According to Dr. Jason Wang, the amended law stipulated the creation of an integrated health command center (an idea developed and shared by the United States before it

---

[89] Source: Remarks by Vice President Chen Chien-Jen. May 7, 2020. Online event titled "Taiwan and the COVID-19 Pandemic: Lessons for the World." Hoover Institution at Stanford University.

dismantled its own center in 2018).[90] A modern command center was duly set up on the top floor of the CDC building in Taipei, replete with a coordination center, a press center, and a lounge for napping. It was upgraded in 2019. The Act also allowed the regulation of traffic and for strict quarantine measures enforced by fines. It enabled the use of public property and land, with compensation, in the pursuit of quarantine. The Act mandated the production and stockpiling of PPE in Taiwan. As a result, Taiwan was able to produce 15 million masks a day by April 2020 and 20 million a day after that.

In terms of the rapid response, a key element was the dispatch to Wuhan of two experts on January 13–14. One of them was Dr. Yin-Ching Chuang, regional commander of the Infectious Diseases Prevention and Treatment Network. The small Taiwan team, along with Hong Kong and Macau colleagues, were invited in Wuhan as part of the long-established medical networks between hospitals on both sides of the Strait. They had lengthy discussions with hospital management and China CDC experts. Much of the discussion centered on whether there was human-to-human transmission. This was initially denied by the Wuhan official chairing their meeting. Then something remarkable happened. Dr. Chuang recalls: "The person from the central government health authority said 'why do [you] give an old conclusion? Now the conclusion is that limited human to human transmission cannot be excluded.' For me that was very important information. I think he [Beijing official] was convinced at least that there was limited human to human transmission. That was my observation. He physically stopped him [the chairperson]."[91] Dr. Chuang concluded: "In my mind that means human to human transmission absolutely." He landed back in Taiwan on January 14. "As soon we landed, the [Taiwan] CDC sent people to meet us at the airport to take us straight to the Director General because the next day [in the] morning he was going to report to his superior. Our government took it very seriously." The Taiwan CDC immediately convened an expert task force and a press conference. The Central Epidemic Command Center (CECC) was activated on January 20, and Taiwan was all systems go.

After January 15, Taiwan rolled out all the measures authorized in its Communicable Disease Control Act. That included rapid restrictions on flights from Wuhan (January 23), later expanded to flights from the rest of China. Patients were triaged at the airports according to levels of risk and travel history.

---

[90] Source: Remarks by Dr. Jason Wong (Stanford Medicine). May 7, 2020. Online event titled "Taiwan and the COVID-19 Pandemic: Lessons for the World." Hoover Institution at Stanford University.

[91] Source: *The Telegraph*. May 6, 2020. "'They wanted to take us sightseeing. I stayed in the hotel', says first foreign official to enter Wuhan." www.telegraph.co.uk/global-health/science-and-disease/wanted-take-us-sight-seeing-stayed-hotel-says-first-foreign/ (last accessed November 30, 2020).

Using Article 48 of the law, the government was also authorized to enforce contact tracing of patients and those suspected to be infected through the sharing of data from cell phone providers.

From January 27, Taiwan went one step further and integrated immigration data with the data system of the national center in order to fully inform the health-care system of potential travel risks. This was an unprecedented big data initiative achieved within one day.[92] This was done on the basis of the public interest exception in the CDC Act, though it was later criticized. A debate has arisen on how to use big data to defeat pandemics, while protecting freedom and privacy. It is likely to require direct stipulation in future legislation.[93]

Strict fourteen-day quarantines were enforced for any returning traveller, replete with mandated COVID-19 safe cars from airport to quarantine spot, daily temperature checks, and reports to the police. However, there was a special Taiwanese soft touch to this: incoming quarantine passengers were given a welcome package with food and toiletry. And Taiwanese citizens (not foreigners) are paid up to US$600 for the two weeks spent in quarantine. This followed a constitutional challenge to the quarantine stipulations. The Constitutional Court issued Interpretation 690, which confirmed the constitutionality of quarantine measures while recognizing their restrictive nature. The Court affirmed that there could be conditions where the sacrifice of personal freedom was necessary for the public good. However, the Court stipulated that quarantine had to be compensated.[94]

With these measures, Taiwan was able to keep schools and businesses open. There were no restrictions on restaurants and bars, public transport, or group gatherings. From Spring 2020, COVID-19 was essentially defeated, with the exception of a few sporadic cases. People were able to live a normal life.

Taiwan's model also relied on rapid, direct, and transparent information, including a daily press conference by the CECC. This helped build trust from the public in the actions taken by the government. Vice President Chen notes that the communication had "a stabilizing influence on society, encouraging citizens to follow rules."[95] He adds: "It is a virtuous cycle: the more public trust,

---

[92] Source: Remarks by Dr. Jason Wong (Stanford Medicine). May 7, 2020. Online event titled "Taiwan and the COVID-19 Pandemic: Lessons for the World." Hoover Institution at Stanford University.

[93] Source: Remarks by Dr. Chang Wen-Chen, Dean, National Chao Tung University Law School. May 7, 2020. Online event titled "Taiwan and the COVID-19 Pandemic: Lessons for the World." Hoover Institution at Stanford University.

[94] Source: Remarks by Dr. Chang Wen-Chen, Dean, National Chao Tung University Law School. May 7, 2020. Online event titled "Taiwan and the COVID-19 Pandemic: Lessons for the World." Hoover Institution at Stanford University.

[95] Source: Remarks by Vice President Chen Chien-Jen. May 7, 2020. Online event titled "Taiwan and the COVID-19 Pandemic: Lessons for the World." Hoover Institution at Stanford University.

the more cooperation. This raises the chances of success." The successes in 2020 are particularly noteworthy because of the contrast with the SARS outbreak of 2003. At that time, people did not understand the need for quarantine and resisted it.

In sum, Taiwan offers a remarkable model of highly effective public policy within a democratic and accountable framework. It is built around reliance on science, trust in government capacity to organize a whole-of-society response, advanced contact-tracing methods, and strict legal stipulations around those tools.

Korea

Korea's actions in response to COVID-19 have followed a broadly similar pattern of high levels of preparedness, strong and early coordination of quarantine and contact-tracing measures, and regular communication. Compared to Taiwan, it kept its border partially open, including with China. Korea also had to deal with pockets of political and social opposition to strong government actions. A large initial cluster took place in the city of Daegu in early February and was linked to the Shincheonji Church of Jesus. By March, however, Korea had largely gained control over COVID-19, although later spikes took place in the summer and late autumn of 2020, featuring some dimensions of political or social resistance.

The Korea Center for Disease Control (KCDC) is the central coordination point for the response. Legal and logistical preparation were much improved in response to the 2015 MERS outbreak, which hit Korea hard and caused thirty-eight deaths (from 184 cases) in the country.[96]

The first Korean feature is rapid response. Through its contacts in China, the KCDC received viral specimens from China prior to January 20. By January 22, Korea set up its centralized emergency response committee. From January 28, travellers with links to Wuhan were subject to monitoring for fourteen days. After February 3, quarantine was enforced by police and local governments. By February 12, the Mask Stabilization Measure came into effect, resulting in a doubling of the production capacity of masks: by March, the average production of masks was 10 million per day.

A second feature has been rapid, massive, and mostly free testing. COVID-19 testing started at local government health facilities on January 31, just eleven days after the first case arrived in Korea. Mass testing in Korea was the result of strong public–private partnerships in the wake of MERS. On January 27, KCDC officials met with infectious disease experts at the Korean Society for Laboratory Medicine and the executives of twenty pharmaceutical companies to start the production of diagnostic test kits. The first private COVID-19 test kit from Kogene Biotech was

---

[96] Source: WHO. www.who.int/westernpacific/emergencies/2015-mers-outbreak.

approved on February 4. A second test kit produced by Seegene Inc. was approved on February 12. Within two weeks of the first case, thousands of test kits were shipped daily. Korea also innovated with the development of rapid drive-through test centers. The first one was established at the Kyungpook National University Chilgok Hospital on February 23.

A third Korean feature has been the large-scale use of systematic contact tracing of positive COVID-19 patients. A first mobile app was introduced for self-diagnosis and monitoring on February 12. A fully GPS-enabled app to enforce the quarantine went live on March 7, with access to location and credit card data to track all contacts of new cases. This involved an unprecedented degree of data gathering but was met with broad social acceptance in the name of public health. The government facilitated the sharing of data among private companies between cell phone companies, credit card companies, and app developers, but it did not take control of the data directly.

A fourth feature is universal health care and government-paid care at hospitals and temporary treatment centers. The government also provided stipends during quarantine.

A fifth feature, as in the case of Taiwan, has been high levels of civic participation, volunteerism, and solidarity in the face of crisis.[97]

Finally, as in the case of Taiwan, Korea's response has featured high-quality communication and transparency. The KCDC leader, Dr. Jeong Eun-kyeong, has earned respect for her work around the clock and regular public briefings, along with President Moon Jae-in. "On the one hand, centered around clear scientific information about the virus, the Ministry of Health and Welfare (MOHW) under Dr. Jung has prioritized educating the public about basic hygiene guidelines (e.g. mask-wearing, handwashing, coughing etiquette) and physical distancing protocols. On the other hand, President Moon has focused on building solidarity amongst Koreans by repeatedly emphasizing the notion of common responsibility. Moon often describes the fight against COVID-19 as a collaborative task whose success rests on good governance and civic cooperation" (Lee, 2020: 92).

Schools closed, but only in a brief period in February–March 2020. Limitations were imposed on group gatherings, but mostly for large or very large groups. Stay-at-home requirements were almost entirely avoided throughout the year (Hale et al., 2020). However, bars and restaurants were shut down in Seoul in April and later again in November (along with churches) during another spike. In August, after a spike in the Seoul bar district, nightclubs and karaoke bars closed. Overall, Korea managed to maintain a high degree of normal social life.

---

[97] Source: Remarks by Dr. Yong Suk Lee. April 24, 2020. Panel titled "Social and Economic Impact of COVID-19 in Asia" at Stanford University's Freeman Spogli Institute.

The success of the Korean government in tackling COVID-19 without shutting down the country or using lockdowns and while maintaining public trust paved the way for a great electoral victory by President Moon on April 15 in the mid-term parliamentary elections. His Democratic Party, in coalition with Together Citizens, swept 60% of the seats, the biggest parliamentary victory for any party since 1987.

Singapore

Singapore[98] relied on similar features of rapid government mobilization, extensive control and contact-tracing measures, and clear and transparent communication to citizens. Because Singapore is such a hub for global travel and trade, it has suffered a bigger economic hit than Taiwan, Korea, or China.

Singapore activated its multi-ministry task force on January 22, the same day as Korea. It involved all relevant ministers from a broad array of domains. It became the single point of entry for decisions and communication. Right from the start, the task force relied on the advice of doctors and health experts from universities and hospitals. By the end of January, Singapore became one of the first few countries to ban all travellers from China, a very unusual move for such a global hub. The government also took immediate measures to guarantee food supplies and control panic-buying. Singapore did use a lockdown (called a "circuit-breaker"), but it was announced and managed carefully to avoid panic or frustrations.

Singapore's response is also marked by a very rigorous and well-organized contact-tracing process. This process was enshrined in law after the SARS epidemic and was well staffed ahead of the crisis. It involves drawing personnel from Ministry of Health staff and police to systematically review all past activities and contacts of suspected cases, including the use of CCTV footage. Remarkably, Singapore releases each day to the entire population (on TV, radio, social media, and mass SMS messages to all citizens) the anonymized summary of all positive cases, including the infection route and locations visited. Confidentiality was guaranteed in the process, and leakers were arrested for leaking confidential information. The goal of such extreme tracking and transparency is to bring the number of cases to zero.[99] The government encouraged testing by committing to cover all related health expenses. Overall, the government's massive communication process earned public support.

---

[98] Special thanks to Jeremy Jee, a Singaporean graduate student at the University of Tokyo.

[99] Additional sources: www.biotechconnection-sg.org/covid-19-contact-tracing/and www.channel newsasia.com/news/singapore/police-missing-link-church-clusters-covid19-coronavirus-12509492.

To be sure, Singapore did rely on enforcement measures as well. To enforce safe physical distancing, the government hired Safe Distancing Ambassadors on a part-time basis, with the mission of patrolling housing estates and malls and ensuring that people were keeping safely apart and were wearing masks. Masks were made mandatory to board any public transport. The government also inspected restaurants and bars.

Within eight weeks of the start of the pandemic, Singapore developed and made available two apps to control the spread of COVID-19. To enter any mall, restaurant, supermarket, or cinema, a QR code called SafeEntry must be scanned, together with a mandatory temperature scan. It is scanned at both entry and exit. This tracks the people in all public establishments and possible contacts with suspected cases. The second is TraceTogether, an open-source Bluetooth contact-tracing app designed to share with the government contact lists of positive COVID-19 cases. It can work on any device, including simple Bluetooth tokens. These tokens contain very limited private information and were designed to protect privacy.

These measures enabled Singapore to limit restrictions on daily life. Schools remained open, group gatherings were not restricted, and lockdowns were limited to affected buildings. However, all bars and cinemas closed on March 26, followed by indoor dining. Restaurants reopened in June.

Singapore encountered some hardships as well. First was its lack of production capacity for face masks, which led to limited availability. There was some controversy about the government keeping the scheduled parliamentary elections in July, in terms of both safety and taking advantage of the pandemic. But the biggest challenge by far was the spread of many cases in a forgotten place: the dormitories for foreign workers on the periphery of the large metropolis. They account for up to 54,000 of the 58,000 cases in Singapore as of November 30, 2020. There are over 1 million foreign workers on limited contracts and low wages in Singapore (out of a population of 5 million). The spread of COVID-19 in crammed dormitories with suboptimal conditions revealed the inequality of pandemics and the hidden side of the Singaporean miracle. The government did announce measures to build more modern dormitories, but these face reactions from taxpayers unwilling to spend public funds on foreigners.

Japan

Japan[100] is a paradoxical case. As illustrated in Table 6, the government response was slower than in the cases explored so far, and the border remained open longer. Quarantine measures and contact-tracing processes were much

---

[100] The author would like to express special thanks to Saya Soma for her able research assistance.

more limited, and the ruling coalition faced disagreement over the social and economic measures necessary to save the economy. The agony of passengers quarantined in Yokohama on the Diamond Princess cruise ship for over two weeks in February exemplified the lack of appropriate and effective measures by the government.[101] There was quite a bit of competition between Prime Minister Abe, seen as slow to act, and Governor Yuriko Koike of Tokyo, who called for more stringent isolation measures to stop the rise of cases. Reliable testing based on the actual detecting of viral RNA (so-called polymerase chain reaction or PCR testing) was slow to ramp up for months and only really increased after July. This low capacity led to overwhelmed health centers and lack of early detection (Shimizu et al., 2020). The Japanese response was also less stringent than those of many other countries and relied on people's self-restraint. Japan did not declare strict lockdown measures with legal enforcement similar to China or Europe. On the Oxford stringency index, Japan hovers between 30 to 40 out of 100 throughout 2020, way below the majority of countries in the world (Hale et al., 2020). Support for intrusive government measures, such as contact-tracing apps, is also lower in Japan that in the rest of East Asia, a legacy of the post-military democratic norms after 1945. Yet, in the end, COVID-19 numbers are low, despite the high elderly proportion and despite a worrying increase between November 2020 and January 2021 and again in Spring 2021.

What saved Japan (at least in 2020) were the strength and universal nature of its health-care system, the universal social practices of mask-wearing and personal hygiene, border controls (as an island nation) after the initial phase, and society's readiness to follow simple recommendations, even without enforcement mechanisms. Japan was also fast to ramp up production of masks and respirators. In March and in the wake of the Diamond Princess disaster, the health authorities understood that the virus was spreading mostly through the air, and the government issued its oft-repeated *san-mitsu* guidelines or "3-Cs": closed spaces, crowded places, and close-contact settings. "In addition to the 3-Cs, the Japanese government warn[ed] of five more specific dangers: dinner parties with booze; drinking and eating in groups of more than four; talking without masks at close quarters; living in dormitories and other small shared spaces; and using changing or break rooms."[102] And while the government measures were mostly voluntary, the fact is that the Japanese population followed the advice.

---

[101] Source: www.ncbi.nlm.nih.gov/pmc/articles/PMC7156812/.

[102] Source: *The Economist.* December 12, 2020. "3-C Epiphany: The Japanese authorities understood COVID-19 better than most." www.economist.com/asia/2020/12/12/the-japanese-authorities-understood-covid-19-better-than-most (last accessed January 23, 2021).

In other words, Japanese cultural habits and behavior played a key role in containing the virus. Deputy Prime Minister Aso boasted about this to other world leaders in diplomatic meetings. He said: "I told these people: 'Between your country and our country, *mindo* (the level of people) is different.' And that made them speechless and quiet."[103]

Estévez-Abe and Ide have revealed another crucial and misunderstood strength in the Japanese response: unlike other countries in North America and Europe with high percentage of elderly populations (where deaths in long-term care facilities [LTCFs] represented a large share of deaths), Japan managed to keep deaths in LTCFs extremely low (Estévez-Abe and Ide, 2021 forthcoming). They argue: "In Japan, this early intervention had little to do with political leadership and top down crisis management. Instead, as this paper demonstrates, it was part of a well-established routine protocol for the prevention and control of communicable diseases in LTCFs" (2). In fact, even Prime Minister Abe was unaware of these automatic procedures taking place. The authors find that "early COVID-19 warnings from the Bureau of Health and Welfare for the Elderly within the Ministry of Health, Labour and Welfare (MHLW) effectively shut down the rest of the LTCFs between mid- and late-February" (5). This was possible due to centralized management of these facilities.

For the rest of society, the response was less effective and has led to interesting debates. Aldrich and Yoshida call the Japanese performance "nothing short of miraculous" and attribute it to social bonding in most parts of Japan. They write: "Japan's pandemic story is that of a country that dodged a bullet without strong leadership from the prime minister, an efficient bureaucracy, or the use of advanced technology. The relatively small number of recorded COVID-19 infections and deaths is likely due to widespread voluntary self-quarantine and a resulting massive reduction in social interactions" (Aldrich and Yoshida, 2020: 220).

In contrast to other East Asian cases reviewed here, the Japanese government's response was slow indeed. There was no activation of a dedicated epidemic control center. On March 8, Professor Murakami Hiromi described the situation in the following words: "The scary truth is that no one is in charge of managing Japan's response to COVID-19. Bureaucrats have failed to put together a competent team or provide transparent reports about decision-making processes. Meanwhile, political leaders make themselves look busy by jumping from meeting to meeting and repeating experts' statements to the

---

[103] Source: BBC. July 3, 2020. www.bbc.com/news/world-asia-53188847.

press instead of making the difficult decisions that are becoming increasingly urgent" (Murakami, 2020).

In fact, the legal tools were initially insufficient, and Japan only amended its Special Law for Epidemics to allow for national emergencies on March 13. At the request of Prime Minister Abe (and without full authority to issue an order), schools closed down on February 26 but reopened on March 20. The timing for reopening, just before cherry blossom gatherings, was poor. On March 25, Governor Koike of Tokyo urged residents to avoid coming out over the weekend, as she saw the cases multiply. Finally, on April 7, the central government issued the State of Emergency declaration for seven prefectures (Tokyo, Kanagawa, Saitama, Chiba, Osaka, Hyogo, and Fukuoka), along with a promise of financial support for lower-income households. The State of Emergency was expanded to thirty-nine prefectures on May 14 and to all of Japan on May 25.

A medical review also found tensions between political leadership and health scientists. Shimizu et al. write:

> Japan's response was also affected by tension between the politics and the science of the pandemic. An expert committee established as a subsidiary of the cabinet was insufficiently independent to provide truly impartial advice. The committee lacked representatives from essential disciplines such as economics, behavioural science, and communication, and decision making processes were poorly explained. For example, the committee's recommendation that social contact should decrease by 80% was later weakened by the government to "a minimum of 70%, or ideally 80%" without further clarification. (Shimizu et al., 2020)

The handling of COVID-19 by the ruling Liberal Democratic Party (LDP) featured tensions between rural and urban interests. With COVID-19 more prevalent in large cities, powerful politicians from rural constituencies emphasized the risk of economic and social losses in rural prefectures. Those included the districts of Abe and some of the most powerful LDP leaders (Aso, Nikai). In April–May, an internal struggle raged about Abe's rushed plan to disburse 300,000 yen (US$2,800) allowances to low-income households. Some members of the LDP (Nikai, the secretary general) and its coalition partner Komeito balked. Abe was forced to backtrack and to settle for a cash handout of 100,000 yen (US$935) to all citizens instead (Mulgan, 2020). He also sent "Abenomasks"[104] to every household in Japan, but this proved ineffective and many were defective.

---

[104] This was a clever play on the wildly successful concept of "Abenomics," but this time it backfired.

One other compromise policy to alleviate the losses for rural areas was the launch of the heavily subsidized "Go To Travel" campaign by the national government on July 22 to encourage travel by urban residents outside big cities. It became controversial during later COVID-19 waves, and it appears to have played a role in spreading COVID-19 to the Hokkaido region. Prime Minister Suga, the champion of this initiative, was forced to abandon it in late autumn of 2020, after suffering a loss of public support partly caused by this policy. In 2021, he remained dogged by criticisms that he had prioritized economic reopening over strict pandemic control.

Minister Nishimura Yasutoshi was appointed on March 6 to lead the Office for Novel Coronavirus Disease Control (under the Cabinet Secretariat) and to manage health communication. However, he has been criticized for a lack of effectiveness in such communication. On November 20, when asked about the reasons for a surge in case numbers, he stated: "Only God knows" (神のみぞ知る).[105]

COVID-19 did exact a high price from Japan. Coinciding with an unrelated illness of Prime Minister Abe, it may have accelerated the downfall of Abe in September. COVID-19 also forced the postponement of the Tokyo Olympics in Summer 2020, an event that the whole nation had focused on for years. The negotiations around the decision to postpone (as opposed to cancel) the Olympics in March–April were a great constraint on the actions of the government. Finally, Japan has paid a severe economic cost and has had to rely on extreme levels of fiscal stimulus and debt to bolster the economy.

As a result of COVID-19, approval for the Abe government went down. In the *Asahi*'s public opinion survey on May 23–24,[106] disapproval for the government's handling of COVID-19 reached 57% (and disapproval for Abe personally 52%). The Edelman study on trust in government on May 28 found that trust went down by 5% in Japan to a low level of 38%.[107] This contrasts to an increase in China (+5% to a total of 95%), India (+6% to a total of 87% in India), Korea (+18% to a total of 67%), or Canada (+20% to a total of 70%). Trust in regional government (54%) is higher than trust in the national government in Japan (38%).

In late 2020 and January 2021, Prime Minister Suga similarly suffered a drop in public support due to weak performance on COVID-19. On December 28, in the face of a surge of cases, Japan declared an entry ban on all foreigners to

---

[105] "「神のみぞ知る」 西村担当相を枝野代表批判," TBS NEWS, November 20, 2020, https://news.tbs.co.jp/newseye/tbs_newseye4132239.html.

[106] "朝日新聞世論調査—質問と回答〈5月23、24日実施〉," 朝日新聞デジタル, May 25, 2020, www.asahi.com/articles/ASN5T0FGVN5SUZPS007.html.

[107] "世界11ヵ国の調査対象国の中で、政府に対する頼度が低下したのは日本のみ," エデルマン ジャパン, June 9, 2020, www.edelman.jp/research/20200609.

Japan. Exceptions were made initially for businesspeople and residents from Korea, China, and nine other Asian countries, but this loophole was closed on January 7, 2021. On the same day, Suga was forced to declare a new one-month limited state of emergency covering Tokyo and neighbouring prefectures with four restrictions: "1) shortening business hours for restaurants and bars, 2) reducing the number of workers at offices by 70%, 3) avoiding outings in the evening, and 4) restrictions on events."[108]

In sum, Japan is a partial outlier in East Asia. It probably underperformed its potential, but the final mortality numbers remained low in 2020 and early 2021. Even though the government was slow to lead the public with effective measures and communication (with the exception of the strong management of long-term care facilities for elderly citizens), the public's own self-restraint and belief in the collective good played a large role. To some extent, Japan also benefited from past investments in health, strong health-care procedures, and past government leadership in previous pandemics. Japan may indeed be the country where universal mask-wearing became commonplace first, going back to the 1918 influenza and the early postwar period.

Mongolia

Mongolia is a remarkable high performer in this crisis, despite a lower health-care capacity. It remained totally COVID-free until November 2020 and scores right alongside Taiwan and Vietnam in the category of lowest deaths per capita. Mongolia achieved this through fast implementation of measures learned from the WHO and others, including the rapid formation of a central command, border closures, and strict lockdown when cases appeared. This enabled Mongolia to hold its parliamentary elections in June, which the incumbent party won in a landslide (Dierkes, 2021).

Other Cases in Southeast Asia

Broadly, Southeast Asia[109] did consistently better than expected by the global health security index presented in Tables 4 and 5, even though Indonesia and the Philippines experienced significantly worse outcomes. Within this region, the leaders in COVID responsiveness are Singapore, Vietnam, Thailand, and Malaysia.

---

[108] Source: *Nikkei Asia*. January 6, 2021. https://asia.nikkei.com/Spotlight/Coronavirus/Japan-s-second-COVID-state-of-emergency-Five-things-to-know (last accessed January 23, 2021).

[109] A remarkable resource for all cases is the Southeast Asia COVID Tracker by CSIS in Washington, DC. www.csis.org/programs/southeast-asia-program/southeast-asia-covid-19-tracker-0.

Given its vulnerable position on the border with China and the memory of SARS, Vietnam was prepared for COVID-19. Within a week of its first case, Vietnam formed a central National Steering Committee for COVID-19, incorporating all twenty-three relevant ministries. The Ministry of Health had set up a hotline by January 27 and a national SMS information system by February 3. It launched a phone app for contact tracing on February 8. It rapidly set up mandatory centralized fourteen-day quarantines for returning travellers and mandatory contact tracing for suspected cases. Mask-wearing became mandatory as well. The province north of Hanoi and bordering China was isolated for three weeks. There was also a national lockdown for twenty-two days in April (including bar and restaurant closures) and further restrictions on group gatherings and bars in August. But Vietnam managed to maintain social life otherwise. Vietnam also innovated with field hospitals and robots to disinfect rooms. Effective communication took place through social media with the spread of a handwashing song gone viral (Duong, 2020).

Vietnam does rely on tough border controls and aggressive control-tracing and information sharing. "In addition to a 14-day quarantine for entrants, [Vietnam] also discloses personal information on newly infected people – such as age, occupation, place of residence and recent activities – for quick tracing of close contacts. This tough response, possible thanks to authoritarian Communist Party rule, has been responsible for keeping cumulative cases down to roughly 1,500."[110]

It is hard to overstate the gains made by Vietnam in 2020, a year when it chaired ASEAN (including the signing ceremony for the RCEP) and experienced booming supply chain relocation from China. It is also important to note that COVID-19 generated hardships and greater inequality for millions of workers who temporarily lost jobs.

Thailand was also quick to act after the first imported cases, including lockdown measures, closing the border with a ban on travel by foreigners on March 22, and contact tracing. Thailand managed to keep school closures and daily life disruptions to a minimum. The WHO singled out Thailand as a success, attributing this to its heavy investments over forty years in a universal health-care system, complemented by one million village health volunteers, and effective communication with the public.[111] However, as noted in Table 6, the economic and social costs have been high and have fueled discontent. The health success of the government with

---

[110] Source: *Nikkei Asia*. January 6, 2021. "Asian trio of Taiwan, Vietnam and Singapore keep COVID near zero." https://asia.nikkei.com/Spotlight/Coronavirus/Asian-trio-of-Taiwan-Vietnam-and-Singapore-keep-COVID-near-zero (last accessed January 23, 2021).

[111] Source: Joe Myers. September 9, 2020. "7 countries we can all learn from to fight future pandemics, according to the WHO." World Economic Forum. www.weforum.org/agenda/2020/09/5-countries-we-can-all-learn-from-to-fight-future-pandemics-according-to-the-who/.

COVID-19 has not assuaged growing public frustrations with the current regime and the powers of the king. Thailand has seen unprecedented protests led by young people, demanding constitutional changes. In January 2021, a major COVID-19 cluster in Bangkok led the government to impose restrictions and close schools in Bangkok and in regions around the capital. The situation was more volatile in early 2021 than in the early phase of the pandemic.

Malaysia has been effective through science-based leadership, contact tracing, lockdown measures, and clear communication. Stewart Nixon writes:

> Malaysia's efforts have been spearheaded by the reassuring leadership of Health Director-General Datuk Dr Noor Hisham Abdullah, whose resume combines a depth of medical knowledge with formidable public policy experience. He and the frontline professionals at the Ministry of Health have been supported by politicians to lead the response rather than being overshadowed by them. Activities have been consistent and nationally synchronised and public messaging clear, factual and accessible across new and old media. A strong and well-resourced public service with depoliticised leadership is proving invaluable. (Nixon, 2020)

Malaysia did impose school closures in March–June 2020. Group gatherings were curbed for periods of time, and a further tightening took place in December 2020–January 2021 (Hale et al., 2020).

Myanmar started COVID with an under-resourced health-care system and high risks. However, during 2020, the country managed to avoid high numbers through very strict and early border controls and quarantine, strong community involvement, and very effective communication centered on the personality of Aung San Suu Kyi as mother of the nation (Wai, 2020). Mobility restrictions and temporary measures were followed and mostly accepted. But Myanmar took a great economic hit with this crisis, and border conflicts are a potential danger (Ostwald and Myint, 2020). Schools were closed in March–July 2020, and group gatherings were restricted (Hale et al., 2020). Limited lockdowns in affected areas were used. By February 1, 2021, however, all hell broke loose in Myanmar with the ruthless military coup launched by General Min Aung Hlaing against the government led by Aung San Suu Kyi in the wake of its landslide re-election in November 2020. Prospects looked bleak for the rest of 2021.

Indonesia has the advantage of a young population, but it has been hampered by limited health capacities (testing in particular) and by the reality of slums, where crowded conditions make tough countermeasures difficult. It created a central COVID-19 Response Acceleration Task Force on March 13 (and disbanded it in July). Travel bans were gradually set up, targeting China first (February) and other high-prevalence countries (March). Schools were closed in the spring, and group gatherings were restricted. On December 28, Indonesia banned all visitors to the country in the face of a surge in cases. The economic and social cost has been much greater. The government estimates that up to 30 million people could be pushed back into poverty.[112] There was much political debate around a large fiscal stimulus plan. Unlike leaders of other Asian countries, President Jokowi is putting a huge priority on rapid, free, and universal access to vaccination.[113] Indonesia is possibly the fastest country with early vaccination, and it has signed a priority vaccine deal with China.

To sum up, governments across East Asia took rapid and effective measures to face COVID-19. These included the creation of emergency coordination units, travel bans, quarantine measures, systematic contact tracing, and coherent communication. These actions built on a specific readiness for pandemics enshrined into law in many countries of the region in the wake of the SARS and MERS epidemics. We also observe general acceptance by the public of either indicative or mandatory measures, even when measures were initially less coherent (as in the case of Japan).

This convergence of reaction measures to COVID-19 can be understood through the activation of similar narratives and historical frames about collective threats and the need for collective measures centered upon the role of a developmental state. The results were strong, with East Asian nations showing very low mortality rates overall.

4 The Surprising Resilience of East Asian Economic Linkages

One of the most striking dimensions of the East Asian response to the COVID-19 pandemic and to the rise of global tensions in 2020 has been the relatively stable relations between the major powers (China–Japan) and the acceleration of regionalism, especially the conclusion of the RCEP. This Asian contribution can be seen as part of a larger trend, given parallel positive trends in Africa and in Europe after a difficult few months. It is also particularly important in the context of the raging debate on the erosion of globalization and uncoupling of economic links from China.

The Debate on the Security of Global Supply Chains during COVID-19

The combination of high dependence by many countries on China for PPE in the midst of a pandemic and rising tensions between Western countries and China has sparked a great debate on the reform of global supply chains. In recent years,

---

[112] Source: www.eastasiaforum.org/2020/06/17/implementing-indonesias-covid-19-stimulus/.
[113] Source: *Nikkei Asia*. December 2020. https://asia.nikkei.com/Spotlight/Coronavirus/Jokowi-pledges-free-COVID-vaccinations-for-all-Indonesians.

global companies moved factories and supplier networks to China and other emerging countries that provided a low-cost but well-educated labor force and good infrastructure. Investment and purchasing decisions were primarily based on price and competitiveness considerations. However, with the USA–China trade war after 2017, the rising use of sanctions or import bans by the United States and China, and increasing security considerations, supply chains are increasingly seen through a security lens. Interdependence can suddenly be weaponized by a stronger player (Farrell and Newman, 2019). Recent examples include actions by China against Canada in 2019 and Australia in 2020 and actions by the United States against Huawei, taking advantage of Huawei's critical dependence on US-designed semi-conductors in 2019–20. The greatest accelerator for this trend was Donald Trump, but the conditions were ready as well.

Razeen Sally argues that the COVID-19 pandemic is happening in a context of increasing state actions, rising unilateralism, and growing geopolitical uncertainty. Such trends are propitious for mercantilism and more political considerations in the pursuit of economic transactions. The pandemic has also made states more risk-averse and eager to be protectionist with respect to medical equipment and electronics. Sally writes: "The reorientation of global value chains will accelerate. Western multinationals will relocate parts of their production from China to other countries on cost grounds, as they have been doing, and increasingly on political-risk and security grounds. There will be a combination of onshoring, near-shoring and regionalisation of value chains, varying by sector. But the overall effect will be to raise costs for producers and consumers" (Sally, 2020).

Over the last three years, there is evidence of many foreign companies moving out of China and of a degree of bifurcation in Asian supply chains.[114] A former high-level Japanese official observed in December 2019: "There is material change taking place in Asia regarding supply chains over the last two years: we gradually see the rise of two clusters of supply chains, one centered around China (and the big Continental market), and one centered around India/ASEAN/Bangladesh. Taiwanese, Japanese, and Korean companies are divesting from China for their exports to the US. But they still invest in China for the China market. The changes in supply chains are amazingly fast.[115]"

Urata Shujiro, a professor at Waseda University, also notes that Japanese car companies suffered from broken supply chains in China during the pandemic and are considering reducing their risks:

---

[114] See Kathrin Hille. October 5, 2020. "The great uncoupling: one supply chain for China, one for everywhere else." *Financial Times.* www.ft.com/content/40ebd786-a576-4dc2-ad38-b97f796b72a0.

[115] Source: Author's personal interview. December 17, 2019.

Japanese firms heavily rely on China for the supply of many goods – including electronics, medical equipment and health products. In recent years, these supply chains have been affected by the US–China trade war and the technology race, as China tries to covertly obtain technology from Japanese and other foreign companies. Diversifying GVCs could involve shortening networks by reducing the number of links in the chain, or by redesigning products to make their components less specific. But these changes are costly which discourages diversification. (Urata, 2020)

In response to such needs, the Japanese government introduced in its Spring 2020 budget a subsidy program to support Japanese companies either to relocate to Japan or to move from China to ASEAN countries and thus reduce Japan's exposure to China. The amounts in 2020 remained modest: 220 billion yen (US$2 billion) for relocation to Japan and 23.5 billion yen (US$200 million) for relocation to ASEAN.

Taiwan launched its New Southbound Policy in 2016 with the goals of reducing its dependence on mainland China and redirecting investments toward ASEAN and India. The Tsai Ing-wen government also launched a three-year reshoring plan to incentivize Taiwanese companies to move back to Taiwan by offering various tax breaks, subsidies, and incentives. The focus is especially on high-tech companies. By Summer 2020, the program attracted pledges by Taiwanese companies to reinvest US$33 billion back to Taiwan (20% of which took place in 2019 with another 33% due to take place in 2020) (Yip, 2020). This reshoring process, along with investments by other foreign companies, likely played a role in the relatively high growth enjoyed by Taiwan.

However, it will take many more years to reduce Taiwan's dependence on the mainland. For example, between 2015 and 2020, the share of exports from Taiwan to mainland China (including Hong Kong) significantly increased from 39% to 44%.[116] During 2020 alone, Taiwan's exports to China increased by 15%. During the second half of 2020, the economic pull of China's relatively quick recovery was being felt by companies in East Asia. The *Nikkei* reported: "Despite a much talked-about 'exit' from China by some, others are staying put."[117] Many companies, such as Komatsu, have seen an unexpectedly high demand increase in China.

---

[116] Source: Taiwan government. http://service.mof.gov.tw/public/Data/statistic/trade/news/10912/ 10912_英文新聞稿.pdf (last accessed February 8, 2021). Special thanks to Jackie Zhao.

[117] Rurika Imahashi and Lauly Li. November 11, 2020. "Japan and Taiwan companies to gain from China's quick recovery." *Nikkei Asia*. https://asia.nikkei.com/Business/Companies/Japan-and-Taiwan-companies-to-gain-from-China-s-quick-recovery?utm_campaign=RN%20Subscriber% 20newsletter&utm_medium=daily%20newsletter&utm_source=NAR%20Newsletter&utm_conte nt=article%20link&del_type=1&pub_date=20201111190000&seq_num=13&si=12476.

At a global level, production value chains held up throughout 2020 better than predicted. Anabel González, former trade minister of Costa Rica and current senior fellow at the Petersen Institute for International Economics (PIIE), wrote a recent memo on the global trading system, which identified surprising resilience:

> Evidence from the first months of the pandemic indicate that global value chains have allowed countries to retain access to diversified sources of medical equipment and thereby strengthen their response capacity. Contrary to a widely accepted view in the early stages of COVID-19, trade is not a problem in the crisis but rather a core element of the solution. (González, 2020)

There is a strong counterargument to the narrative of an easy and rapid move of global supply chains from China, given the scale of the Chinese economy relative to India and Southeast Asia. Shiro Armstrong writes: "Economic distancing from China or self-isolation will both deepen the economic crisis and prolong the path towards recovery. It will not make supply chains more resilient. It would also represent a geopolitical catastrophe for both sides, reducing China's stake in an open global order, creating enmity where none need exist" (Armstrong, 2020).

From his vantage point in Singapore and Indonesia, Christian Bachheimer argues: "Despite the rhetoric of self-reliance and the return of domestic manufacturing, no single country can produce the whole set of activities facilitated by [global value chains (GVCs)]. GVCs and their primary clusters are sticky due to high fixed costs and immense economies of scale that stubbornly resist decoupling by external forces with competing locations" (Bachheimer, 2020). He adds that countries such as Vietnam and Indonesia do not have the scale and infrastructure to host massive relocations from China. He states that supply chain diversification and reliance on international rules and institutions are the best protectors of national interest. This is a dominant view in Asia.

In sum, geopolitical risks have definitely increased in Asia and many global companies have started to develop China+1 or China+2 strategies to lower their exposures. In 2020 and 2021, the Chinese economic gravity pull remained large, and large-scale decoupling appeared unrealistic to most global players. However, should a major security crisis in the Taiwan Strait or South China Sea happen, it would likely wreak havoc with these expectations.

Continued East Asian Support for Regional Integration and Globalization

As the COVID-19 pandemic grew ever more powerful and divisive in February–April 2020, debates raged about the likely rise of protectionism and risks for the poorly institutionalized East Asian regionalism.

What is striking, however, is how much East Asian countries saw the pandemic as a common threat that required more cooperation and multilateralism, including in trade. In conversations in Japan, Korea, and Southeast Asia over the last two years, I have been struck by the amount of elite and grassroot support for continued economic integration, which is linked to economic progress and middle-class success in much of East Asia. There may be support for security adjustments with China but not for wholesale decoupling or conflict.

Hoang Oanh, deputy director of the Center for Regional and Foreign Policy Studies at the Institute of Foreign Policy and Strategic Studies of the Diplomatic Academy of Vietnam, issued a call for "a stronger commitment to multilateralism." He argued: "The COVID-19 pandemic is demonstrating that a single disease can cause more catastrophic damage than wars and conflicts. The crisis makes it painfully clear that a transnational threat requires a transnational response. But international cooperation has been mostly limited to the sharing of medical equipment and expertise. Multilateral efforts have been impeded by the return of nationalism and great power rivalry" (Oanh, 2020).

At the opening ceremony of the Jeju Forum for Peace and Prosperity on November 6, 2020, President Moon Jae-in of Korea emphasized common aspirations for "inclusiveness and coexistence." Former Singapore prime minister Goh Chok Tong denounced "zero-sum game" approaches that can trample all other countries in the region, adding: "Everyone should speak up against unilateralism and advocate multilateralism and rule of law."

RCEP: A Powerful Counter-Signal In the Midst of a Pandemic

The digital signing ceremony of the RCEP on November 15, 2020, by thirteen leaders of East Asian countries (all except Mongolia and East Timor), as well as the leaders of Australia and New Zealand, was a powerful and symbolic moment. With the stroke of their pens, the fifteen leaders signaled that, despite populism in the West, despite the pandemic, and despite USA–China tensions, they were moving forward with further economic integration within a region that represents 30% of the world's population and economic activity. True, they were disappointed that India, the sixteenth member in the negotiations, chose not to join RCEP. True also, RCEP rules are shallower than those created by the Comprehensive and Progressive Trans-Pacific Partnership (CPTPP), especially with regards to investment rules, public procurement, environment protection, labor protection, and progressive dimensions (gender and indigenous rights in particular).

Nonetheless, there is more to the RCEP than meets the eye. The RCEP is expected to offer a significant boost to regional supply chains because of its single rules of origins certificate for the entire region, with very generous terms and various options.

Leaders in Southeast Asia were particularly enthusiastic about the boost provided by the RCEP to growth prospects. Petri and Plummer argue that RCEP and CPTPP together "forcefully stimulate *intra*-East Asian integration around China and Japan. This is partly the result of U.S. policies" (Petri and Plummer, 2020). The authors calculate that the RCEP will more than offset the costs of the USA–China trade war for all signatories except China. As well, "RCEP and the CPTPP are powerful counterexamples to the global decline in rules-based trade."

The fact that these fifteen leaders could spare focus and time to conclude the eight years of protracted negotiations on RCEP in the midst of COVID-19's huge second wave in Europe and the Americas reminds the world that they have mostly controlled the virus. They are looking forward to the post-pandemic geo-economic game.

Above all, the RCEP means continued momentum for globalization in Asia, including China. Despite their growing wariness (or even, in the case of Australia, outright conflict) with China, Southeast nations, Japan, Korea, Australia, and New Zealand believe in the importance of trade and connectivity for their own prosperity. They all wish to increase trade with each other. But they also know that they cannot guarantee their economic prosperity without stable and regularized trade relations with China. Even Vietnam, the greatest winner from the USA–China trade war, relies heavily on imports of intermediary products from China.

Another key point about the RCEP is that it embeds the very first trilateral FTA between China, Korea, and Japan and opens the door for a possible further CJK agreement in years to come. In essence, the three countries are saying that their common economic interest can trump their current geopolitical and security tensions. But it was also easier to achieve because ASEAN was in the driver seat. The Korean press coverage of RCEP's signature emphasized the increased trade with ASEAN and with the broader region, rather than trade with China or Japan.[118] Interestingly, the European Union's official response also emphasized ASEAN and the rules-based order.[119] As for China, the official commentary emphasized a victory for free trade and for multilateralism.[120]

---

[118] Sources: https://news.naver.com/main/read.nhn?mode=LSD&mid=sec&sid1=101&oid=001&aid=0012015359; https://n.news.naver.com/article/055/0000770600; www.hani.co.kr/arti/economy/marketing/970126.html.

[119] Source: https://eeas.europa.eu/headquarters/headquarters-homepage/88997/regional-comprehensive-economic-partnership---what-does-it-mean-eu_en.

[120] Source: Xinhuanet. http://en.people.cn/n3/2020/1116/c90000-9780701.html.

The RCEP was ASEAN-initiated and ASEAN-led since 2012, but Japan was possibly the true pivotal player. And it is particularly striking that Japan signed the RCEP, which embeds its first FTA with China, at the same time as it plays a vigorous role in the Quad, the security network with the United States, Australia, and India. Japan hosted the Quad Foreign Minister summit in Tokyo on October 6, 2020 and joined the Malabar naval exercises later that month. Japan is also actively pursuing its Free and Open Indo Pacific Strategy (FOIP). However, Japan is pursuing a parallel strategy of security hedging against China and pragmatic economic engagement with China, given its geographical position. For Abe and Suga, the RCEP is part of a series of other global and regional institutional initiatives designed to reduce global risks and buttress the liberal international order (Tiberghien et al., 2020). The RCEP was always seen as the final component in Abe's larger global economic strategy, alongside the CPTPP, the EU–Japan partnership, and the bilateral deal with the United States.

With China, Japan has concluded that decoupling is impossible and that the relationship must be managed with a bundle of cooperation and deterrence. For example, Professor Kitaoka Shinichi, former Japanese UN ambassador and president of the Japan International Cooperation Agency, recently discussed the great risks of domination posed by the rise of China and the necessity of buttressing deterrence. Yet, in the same discussion, he added that East Asian economic construction was still a goal for everyone in Asia, including reforms, cooperation, and trade. He also said: "Japan is a frontline state between the US and China," noting that Japan would suffer great damage if things went wrong. "We cannot take as harsh a position as the US. The majority of people keep quiet. They hope for a good way to stabilize the relationship with China."[121]

Japan is carefully seeking to manage its exposure with China. But China (including Hong Kong) still absorbs 25% of Japanese exports, significantly ahead of the United States (19%).[122] When negotiating its own bilateral trade agreement with the USA in the summer of 2019, Japan was careful to avoid any clause that would limit its ability to complete the RCEP with China in its midst – or any future trilateral agreement with China and Korea. Indeed, Japan had watched the United States impose such a clause on Canada and Mexico, which prevents them from entering into either a bilateral or a multilateral trade

---

[121] Source: Public presentation at the October 13, 2020, webinar at Stanford University titled "Japan's Foreign Policy Options in the Changing Asia-Pacific" (as part of the Shorenstein APARC's fall webinar series "Shifting Geopolitics and U.S.–Asia Relations").

[122] Source: IMF. Direction of Trade Statistics. Data table "Exports and Imports by Areas and Countries," DOTS. http://data.imf.org/?sk=9D6028D4-F14A-464C-A2F2-59B2CD424B85&sId=1409151240976 (last accessed August 31, 2020).

agreement with China or with other non-market economies without US author-
ization (Article 32:10 in the new USMCA agreement, known as NAFTA 2.0). It
was well known that the Trump administration was seeking to introduce such
poison pills in all the bilateral agreements it was signing with its partners.
"Japan cannot accept such a clause in its bilateral deal with the US because of
RCEP (and CJK). RCEP is too important for us."[123] For Japan, the RCEP brings
more legalization to its trade with China in areas such as e-commerce (including
provisions supporting consumer protection and banning the requirement of data
localization), government procurement, intellectual property rights, and rules of
origins. These provisions go beyond WTO rules. Japan has also been consistent
to stand for principles of openness and rule of law, which are enshrined in the
RCEP.

China–Japan Cooperation during the COVID-19 Pandemic

In the midst of USA–China tensions and the chaos from COVID-19 – and
following periods of great tensions in 2011–13 – bilateral Sino-Japanese relations experienced something very unusual: a high degree of stability and even
expressions of mutual compassion throughout 2020. This stable relationship at
the heart of Asia has played a large role in enabling the RCEP and supporting
East Asia's response to the pandemic. It is also noteworthy that the Chinese
ambassador in Japan, Kong Xuanyou, belongs to the more pragmatic faction of
the foreign minister and has not acted as a "wolf warrior diplomat."

Early in the crisis, Japan sent shipments of masks and other goods to China,
gestures that were deeply appreciated by the Chinese, from the elite to the
common people. They became a key topic in Chinese social media circles.
Cheng Li and Ryan McElween report unusual spontaneous events early in the
pandemic:

> The Japanese government was quick to take symbolic action, with members
> of Japan's ruling Liberal Democratic Party voting to donate 5,000 yen
> (around $45) each from their monthly salaries – totaling 2 million yen or
> $18,170 – to help fight the outbreak in China. The Japanese government built
> on those efforts by sending thousands of pieces of protective garments to
> Wuhan, while the residents of Oita prefecture – Japanese sister city of
> Wuhan – also gifted 30,000 masks to the epicenter of the coronavirus.
> Other cities, including Mito, Okayama and Maizuru, joined the effort. (Li
> and McElveen, 2020)

The Chinese foreign minister's official spokesperson, Geng Shuang, addressed
these gifts with the following words – again, very unusual: "After the epidemic

---

[123] Source: Author's interview with senior government adviser in Tokyo. December 16, 2019.

struck, the Japanese government and people provided valuable support and assistance to China at the earliest time possible. We will remember and hold dear such friendship. The Chinese people are also following the spread of the virus in Japan with care and concern. We completely relate to what they are going through. To quote a line from the Book of Songs, "You throw a peach to me, I give you a white jade for friendship."[124]

When Prime Minister Abe announced that he was stepping down in August, the Chinese Foreign Ministry's spokesman, Zhao Lijian (normally known for his wolf warrior remarks), had exceptionally positive words to say:

> In recent years, China–Japan relations got back to the right track and achieved new progress. Leaders of the two sides reached important consensus on building a bilateral relationship in keeping with the new era. We speak positively of Prime Minister Abe's important efforts in this process and wish him a speedy recovery.
>
> We stand ready to work together with the Japanese side to stay committed to the principles and spirit established in the four political documents and deepen anti-epidemic and socioeconomic cooperation to ensure the sustained improvement and development of China–Japan relations.[125]

The relative stabilization of Japan–China relations in 2020 follows some break-throughs that took place at the Japan-led Osaka G20 Summit in June 2019. In their bilateral meetings before the Summit, Abe and Xi agreed upon a ten-point bilateral agreement, which included support for the RCEP and cooperation in investments in Southeast Asia. At the G20 and against initial odds, China signed on to the Japan-led Quality Infrastructure Platform in part championed by Abe to push back against low-quality infrastructure investment in the BRI. Furthermore, at the Osaka G20, China agreed to sign both the OECD principles on artificial intelligence and the declaration on free data flows with trust advanced by Abe. Ironically, the so-called Osaka Track on data failed due to opposition by India, Indonesia, and South Africa (eager to retain the right to protect their infant digital industry).

Also important is the convergence of China, Japan, and Korea in September 2020 around their pledges of net carbon neutrality by 2050 (Japan, Korea) or 2060 (China). All three rival countries have converged in their understanding of the climate menace and of the urgency to move on with green technology. All three countries (and others in the region) can increasingly be characterized as eco-developmental states (Esarey et al., 2020).

---

[124] Source: www.fmprc.gov.cn/mfa_eng/xwfw_665399/s2510_665401/2511_665403/t1748036.shtml.

[125] Source: www.fmprc.gov.cn/mfa_eng/xwfw_665399/s2510_665401/t1810552.shtml.

Japan–China people-to-people ties have also greatly increased in recent years, with an increase of Chinese tourists in Japan from 1.3 million in 2013 to 9.6 million in 2019 (Li and McElveen, 2020). These trends all go against years of tensions and acrimony.

In a sense, Japan and China may have started an experiment in hedged institutional engagement, combining security markers with support for regional and global institutions. This experiment is fragile and was enabled by Abe's strong leadership. It took place against the background of extremely low levels of Japanese trust in China and high vulnerability to events in the region and actions taken by either the United States or China. And tensions around the disputed Diaoyu/Senkaku islands administered by Japan continued unabated, including regular Chinese Coast Guard intrusions in the zone (except in September 2020, the month when Abe stepped down). The improvements were nonetheless noteworthy. In the midst of the great COVID-19 crisis of 2020, Sino-Japanese relations were remarkably stable. By 2021, the mood had changed, and relations between China and Japan became tense. During the April 2021 Biden–Suga summit, Japan and the United States gave significant attention to the China threat and included a sensitive mention of the Taiwan Strait in their joint statement. Security concerns rose to the fore. The future will tell if the 2020 stability was just an outlier event.

Convergence Between the China-Led AIIB and Japan-Led ADB during the Pandemic

Another dimension of pragmatic cooperation in East Asia relates to the actions of the two rival development banks. The Asian Development Bank (ADB) is the long-established bank based in Manila and has always been led by a Japanese official. The Asian Infrastructure Investment Bank (AIIB) is the upstart created by China in 2014 with a focus on infrastructure. In the end, China developed high-quality statutes and an international board that includes many developed countries.

Interestingly, the AIIB effected a major policy shift during the COVID-19 pandemic and decided to devote its available funds to support Asian countries in their health emergency with COVID. In so doing, the AIIB converged with the actions taken by the ADB as well, actions that were in tune with the long-time presence of the ADB in health.

In March 2020, the ADB announced a $6.5 billion package for health emergencies in the region. On April 2, 2020, the AIIB announced that it would lend at least $5 billion to Asian countries struggling with the pandemic. Jin Liqun, president of the AIIB, said: "The crisis has laid bare the vulnerability of so many countries. We need to focus on building up the public health infrastructure."[126]

According to data tracked by the Center for Strategic and International Studies in Washington DC, by November 2020 the ADB ended up disbursing $13.2 billion in COVID-19 aid and the AIIB $6.7 billion, for a joint total of $20 billion (Segal and Henderson, 2020). Table 7 lists the top recipients for both banks as of November 16. We find Indonesia, Philippines, India, and Kazakhstan among the top five recipients for both banks.

These results would not have been predicted at the time of the creation of the AIIB. They manifest the degree of convergence and cooperation within the East Asian region during COVID-19.

5 Conclusion

The COVID-19 pandemic has caused a massive health, economic, and geopolitical shock to the world. Taking place in the context of great power tensions between the United States and China and of a Trump administration that had turned away from multilateralism, the COVID-19 disruption did not lead to a burst of international cooperation. Instead, the world experienced fragmentation and tensions within global health and global economic institutions. In the fog of the pandemic, both the United States and China took aggressive actions toward each other and toward others. Misperceptions and tit-for-tat accusations and sanctions multiplied. China launched a harsh legal crackdown on Hong Kong in June 2020, while accelerating its harsh repression and incarceration of Uyghur people in Xinjiang. In May, China became embroiled in a deadly high-altitude border conflict with India. The United States fought with the WHO and with allies over multilateralism and climate change.

Different people around the world interpreted the COVID-19 crisis through different narratives. In times of uncertainty, societies seek meaning and rely on past experiences to provide those meanings. They build on culture and history to provide guidance for the present. The problem, of course, is that the rise of national narratives generates parallel realities and parallel interpretations. At best, these narratives are misunderstood by other players and generate misperceptions. At worst, narratives of the others create a sense of threat and trigger a kind of fight-or-flight behavior. This clash of narratives clearly happened between the United States and China. The USA saw this as a foreign virus and read the events through a lens focused on preserving freedom and the American way of life. China saw the virus as another historic calamity that necessitated the

---

[126] Source: Henny Sender and James Kynge. "AIIB and ADB to lend billions in battle against coronavirus." *Financial Times*. April 2, 2020. www.ft.com/content/1f13dcce-b590-43e9-a15b -188f3f3b966b.

Table 7 Top 15 recipients of COVID-19 aid from the ADB and the AIIB
(November 16, 2020)

	ADB recipients	$ (million)	AIIB recipients	$ (million)
1	Philippines	1843	India	1250
2	India	1518	Indonesia	1000
3	Indonesia	1518	Kazakhstan	750
4	Thailand	1500	Philippines	750
5	Kazakhstan	1003	Pakistan	750
6	Pakistan	853	Turkey	583
7	Uzbekistan	629	China	356
8	Bangladesh	612	Bangladesh	350
9	Myanmar	280	Russian Federation	300
10	Nepal	253	Georgia	154
11	Cambodia	250	Uzbekistan	100
12	Mongolia	206	Vietnam	100
13	Regional Companies	200	Mongolia	100
14	Georgia	100	Kyrgyz Republic	50
15	Tajikistan	53	Fiji	50

full mobilization of state and society, as well as international cooperation. When attacked, it reacted with anger and emotion.

Yet, in the midst of this challenging year, interesting developments took place in East Asia. Nearly all countries in the larger East Asian region, whether democracies or autocracies, reacted with a high degree of concordance and effectiveness that led them to control the virus more effectively than elsewhere. While the rest of the world struggled, East Asia experienced heightened regional cooperation. This cooperation culminated in the signing of the largest free trade deal in the world, the RCEP, on November 15, 2020.

This outcome is puzzling, given East Asia's history of weak institutionalization and significant cleavages. Theoretically, a loosely institutionalized region would seem more liable to fragmentation. Cooperation under loose coupling, intense cultural differences, diverging political and security values, and various levels of development is a puzzling outcome. This is a hard case for cooperation and an interesting test case for the survival of civilization under global disruptions. Does the East Asian trajectory during COVID-19 offer clues for how humanity can deal with future catastrophes and challenges?

Within the debate on regionalism in world politics, scholars have often contrasted East Asian processes with European institution-building. While Europe followed an ever-tightening logic of functionalism (Schmitter, 2005) with a growing array of powerful institutions and even a common Central Bank, Asia eschewed legalism and pursued a softer pathway of "talk shops," declarations, and roadmaps. Writing about ASEAN, Mahbubani and Sng describe its process as a "living laboratory of peaceful civilizational coexistence" (Mahbubani and Sng, 2017: 1).

Despite powerful and ever-growing business and human networks in the region, led by the Chinese diaspora, Japanese corporations, Korean companies, Singaporean and Vietnamese companies, and the new Chinese-led Belt and Road Initiative (BRI), there is no overarching Asian Union or Asian economic union. The closest we have to a pan–East Asian/Oceanian economic institution is the RCEP, created in November 2020, in the midst of the pandemic! East Asia and Asia as a whole embody a paradox of liberal integration without institutions. Yet, so far, East Asia has also witnessed a high degree of stability and support for economic integration, despite political and security dangers. What has driven Asian integration over recent decades?

This Element has argued that three factors can elucidate this dual East Asian COVID-19 paradox.

First, the domestic successes of individual countries with the pandemic have been driven by high institutional capacity. Second, most East Asian (and Oceanian) nations showed high levels of social cohesion, preparation, and capacity to act collectively. Third, the increase in regional cooperation in 2020 in spite of pandemic tensions is the result of the reinforcement of a strategic choice for regional integration and a rules-based order in the face of a collective situational threat. Despite their great differences, East Asian nations share similar institutional designs and economic interests.

As we come out of the COVID-19 crisis, we are likely to witness a similar collective focus and regional reinforcement around green technologies and climate actions across East Asia. This is not just because of an acute sense of threat. East Asian nations already compete for pole position in the future green economy that they calculate will replace our current model in the 2030s. This time, the United States – led by the Biden administration – Europe, and many other actors are actively joining the race to help usher in a better global future. Common visions around societal goals and norms of mutual toleration may hold the clue to humanity's ability to tackle future mega-risks.

The COVID-19 shock to humanity was painful. Yet, ultimately, it primarily served as a warning. Humanity is more advanced than ever before. But it will face more deadly pandemics and the systemic risks of a potential devastating climate reality after 2050. The COVID-19 crisis has taught us that our public policy institutions and global governance capacities must up their games fast in order to face these challenges. The good news is that good practices already exist and that game-changing innovations are within our reach. It is just a matter of common vision, cooperation, and mutual respect.

References

Akamatsu K (1962) A historical pattern of economic growth in developing countries. *Journal of Developing Economies* 1(1): 3–25.

Aldrich D and Yoshida T (2020) How Japan stumbled into a pandemic miracle. *Current History* 119: 217–221.

Alvelda P, Ferguson T, and Mallery JC (2020) To save the economy, save people first. *Institute for New Economic Thinking.* www.ineteconomics.org/perspec tives/blog/to-save-the-economy-save-people-first.

Armstrong S (2020) Economic distancing from China and the world would carry heavy costs. *East Asia Forum.* www.eastasiaforum.org/2020/06/07/ economic-distancing-from-china-and-the-world-would-carry-heavy-costs/.

Arnold C (2018) *Pandemic 1918: Eyewitness Accounts from the Greatest Medical Holocaust in Modern History.* New York: St Martin's Press.

Bachheimer C (2020) Global value chains aren't going anywhere. *East Asia Forum.* www.eastasiaforum.org/2020/07/17/global-value-chains-arent-going-anywhere/.

Barrett S (2007) *Why Cooperate? The Incentive to Supply Global Public Goods.* Oxford; New York: Oxford University Press.

Barro RJ, Ursua JF, and Weng J (2020) The coronavirus and the great influenza epidemic: lessons from the "Spanish Flu" for the coronavirus's potential effects on mortality and economic activity. www.aei.org/wp-content/uploads/2020/03/ Barro-coronavirus-Great-Influenza-WP.pdf (accessed November 23, 2020).

Berman P (2020) *Upstream Drivers of Effective Pandemic Response: An Initiative at UBC to Learn How to Better Engage the Institutional, Organizational, Governance, and Political Factors that Determine Success.* Vancouver: University of British Columbia.

Calder KE (2019) *Super Continent: The Logic of Eurasian Integration.* Stanford, CA: Stanford University Press.

Calder KE and Fukuyama F (2008) *East Asian Multilateralism: Prospects for Regional Stability.* Baltimore, MD: Johns Hopkins University Press.

Calder KE and Ye M (2010) *The Making of Northeast Asia.* Stanford, CA: Stanford University Press.

Christakis NA (2020) *Apollo's Arrow: The Profound and Enduring Impact of Coronavirus on the Way We Live.* New York: Little, Brown Spark.

Dierkes J (2021) Mongolia weathers the storms of 2020. *East Asia Forum.* www .eastasiaforum.org/2021/01/14/mongolia-weathers-the-storms-of-2020/.

Drezner DW (2014) *The System Worked: How the World Stopped Another Great Depression*. Oxford: Oxford University Press.

Duong MC (2020) Lessons from Vietnam's COVID-19 victories. *East Asia Forum*. www.eastasiaforum.org/2020/04/21/lessons-from-vietnams-covid-19-victories/.

Eichengreen B (2020) The geopolitical contours of a post-COVID-19 world. *East Asia Forum*. www.eastasiaforum.org/2020/05/02/the-geopolitical-contours-of-a-post-covid-19-world/.

Elliott DSP and Poth J (1983) *Saltwater People: A Resource Book for the Saanich Native Studies Program*. Saanich, BC: Saanich School District.

Emmerson DK (2020) *The Deer and the Dragon: Southeast Asia and China in the 21st Century*. Stanford, CA: Walter H. Shorenstein Asia-Pacific Research Center.

Esarey A, Haddad MA, Lewis JI, and Harrell S (2020) *Greening East Asia: the Rise of the Eco-Developmental State*. Seattle: University of Washington Press.

Estévez-Abe M and Ide H (2021 forthcoming) COVID-19 and Japan's small death toll in long-term care facilities. *Journal of Aging and Social Policy*. https://programs.wcfia.harvard.edu/files/us-japan/files/margarita_estevez-abe_covid19_and_japanese_ltcfs.pdf.

Farrell H and Newman AL (2019) Weaponized interdependence: How global economic networks shape state coercion. *International Security* 44(1): 42–79.

Gerschenkron A (1962) *Economic Backwardness in Historical Perspective*. Cambridge, MA: Belknap Press.

Goh E (2020) The Asia Pacific's "Age of Uncertainty:" Great Power Competition, Globalisation, and the Economic-Security Nexus. *RSIS Working Paper Series*. www.rsis.edu.sg/wp-content/uploads/2020/06/WP330.pdf (accessed June 27, 2020).

Goh E and Prantl J (2020) COVID-19 is exposing the complexity of connectivity. *East Asia Forum*. www.eastasiaforum.org/2020/04/08/covid-19-is-exposing-the-complexity-of-connectivity/.

González A (2020) Memorandum on priorities to revitalize the World Trade Organization. *Rebuilding the Global Economy*. www.piie.com/sites/default/files/documents/gonzalez-2020-11-rtge-memo.pdf

Hale T, Webster S, Petherick A, et al. (2020) *Oxford COVID-19 Government Response Tracker*. Oxford: Blavatnik School of Government.

Harari YN (2020) The world after coronavirus. *Financial Times*. www.ft.com/content/19d90308-6858-11ea-a3c9-1fe6fedcca75.

Hiebert M (2020a) COVID-19 threatens democracy in Southeast Asia. *East Asia Forum*. www.eastasiaforum.org/2020/05/25/covid-19-threatens-democracy-in-southeast-asia/.

Hiebert M (2020b) *Under Beijing's Shadow: Southeast Asia's China Challenge.* Lanham, MD; Boulder, CO; New York; London: Rowman & Littlefield.

Horton R (2020) *The COVID-19 Catastrophe: What's Gone Wrong and How to Stop It Happening Again.* Cambridge, UK; Medford, MA: Polity Press.

Ikenberry GJ (2011) *Liberal Leviathan: The Origins, Crisis, and Transformation of the American World Order.* Princeton, NJ: Princeton University Press.

Ikenberry GJ (2018) The end of liberal international order? *International Affairs* 41(1): 7–23.

Irwin DA (2020) The pandemic adds momentum to the deglobalization trend. *Realtime Economics Issues Watch.* www.piie.com/blogs/realtime-economic-issues-watch/pandemic-adds-momentum-deglobalization-trend?utm_sour ce=update-newsletter&utm_medium=email&utm_campaign=piie-insider (accessed May 30, 2020).

Jia Q (2020) China's diplomatic response to COVID-19. *East Asia Forum.* www .eastasiaforum.org/2020/05/17/chinas-diplomatic-response-to-covid-19/.

Johnson CA (1982) *MITI and the Japanese Miracle: The Growth of Industrial Policy, 1925–1975.* Stanford, CA: Stanford University Press.

Kagan R (2018) *The Jungle Grows Back: America and Our Imperiled World.* New York: Alfred A. Knopf.

Kahneman D (2011) *Thinking, Fast and Slow.* Toronto: Doubleday Canada.

Katzenstein PJ and Shiraishi T (1997) *Network Power: Japan and Asia.* Ithaca, NY: Cornell University Press.

Khanna P (2019) *The Future Is Asian: Commerce, Conflict, and Culture in the 21st Century.* New York: Simon & Schuster.

Khong YF and Nesadurai HES (2007) Hanging together, institutional design, and cooperation in South East Asia: AFTA and the ARF. In Acharya A and Johnston AI (eds), *Crafting Cooperation: Regional International Institutions in Comparative Perspective*, pp. 32–82. New York: Cambridge University Press.

Kuik C-C (2008) The essence of hedging: Malaysia and Singapore's response to a rising China. *Contemporary Southeast Asia* 30(2): 159–185.

Kuik C-C (2020) Hedging in post-pandemic Asia: What, how, and why? *The Asian Forum*, 8. www.theasanforum.org/hedging-in-post-pandemic-asia-what-how-and-why/ (accessed November 23, 2020).

Larsen CA (2014) Social cohesion: Definition, measurement and developments. Report: Institut for Statskundskab, Aalborg Universitet. www.un.org/esa/socdev/egms/docs/2014/LarsenDevelopmentinsocialcohesion.pdf.

Lee Y (2020) South Korea. In Tworek H, Beacock I, and Ojo E (eds), *Democratic Health Communications during COVID-19: A RAPID Response.* Vancouver: SPPGA (UBC).

Li B and Lu B (2020) How China made its COVID-19 lockdown work. *East Asia Forum*. www.eastasiaforum.org/2020/04/07/how-china-made-its-covid -19-lockdown-work/.

Li C and McElveen R (2020) Mask diplomacy: How coronavirus upended generations of China–Japan antagonism. www.brookings.edu/blog/order- from-chaos/2020/03/09/mask-diplomacy-how-coronavirus-upended-gener ations-of-china-japan-antagonism/ (accessed May 31, 2020).

Liu Z, Ciais P, Deng Z, et al. (2020) Near-real-time monitoring of global CO_2 emissions reveals the effects of the COVID-19 pandemic. *Nature Communications* 11(1): article number 5172.

Mackenzie D (2020) *COVID-19: The Pandemic that Never Should Have Happened and How to Stop the Next One*. New York: Hachette.

Mahbubani K and Sng J (2017) *The ASEAN Miracle: A Catalyst for Peace*. Singapore: National University of Singapore Press.

Mulgan AG (2020) COVID-19 highlights Abe's leadership failings. *East Asia Forum*. www.eastasiaforum.org/2020/05/05/covid-19-highlights-abes- leadership-failings/.

Murakami H (2020) A Japan divided over COVID-19 control. *East Asia Forum*. www.eastasiaforum.org/2020/03/08/a-japan-divided-over-covid-19-control/.

Nayyar D (2019) *Resurgent Asia: Diversity in Development*. Oxford: Oxford University Press.

Nixon S (2020) Malaysia beats brutal COVID-19 expectations. *East Asia Forum*. www.eastasiaforum.org/2020/04/30/malaysia-beats-brutal-covid -19-expectations/.

Nye A (2020) The G20's impasse on Special Drawing Rights (SDRs). https:// som.yale.edu/blog/the-g20-s-impasse-on-special-drawing-rights-sdrs.

Oanh H (2020) COVID-19 demands a stronger commitment to multilateralism. *East Asia Forum*. www.eastasiaforum.org/2020/05/12/covid-19-demands -a-stronger-commitment-to-multilateralism/

Okimoto D (1989) *Between MITI and the Market*. Stanford, CA: Stanford University Press.

Osterholm MT and Olshaker M (2017) *Deadliest Enemy: Our War Against Killer Germs*. New York: Little, Brown and Company.

Osterholm MT and Olshaker M (2020) *Deadliest Enemy: Our War Against Killer Germs (2020 Edition)*. New York: Little, Brown and Company.

Ostwald K and Myint T (2020) COVID in Myanmar – IDRC Newsletter.

Pempel TJ (2005) *Remapping East Asia: The Construction of a Region*. Ithaca, NY: Cornell University Press.

Petri PA and Plummer M (2020) RCEP: A new trade agreement that will shape global economics and politics. *Order from Chaos*. www.brookings.edu/blog/

order-from-chaos/2020/11/16/rcep-a-new-trade-agreement-that-will-shape-global-economics-and-politics/.

Quick JD (2018) *The End of Epidemics: The Looming Threat to Humanity and How to Stop It.* New York: St Martin's Press.

Rudd K (2020) The coming post-COVID anarchy: The pandemic bodes ill for both American and Chinese power – and for the global order. *Foreign Affairs* (May 6).

Sally R (2020) Trade, deglobalisation and the new mercantilism. *East Asia Forum.* www.eastasiaforum.org/2020/07/11/trade-deglobalisation-and-the-new-mercantilism/.

Schmitter PC (2005) Ernst B. Haas and the legacy of neofunctionalism. *Journal of European Public Policy* 12(2): 255–272.

Segal S and Henderson J (2020) International financial institutions' COVID-19 approvals decline even as G20 leaders call for additional support. *Commentary.* www.csis.org/analysis/international-financial-institutions-covid-19-approvals-decline-even-g20-leaders-call (accessed November 30, 2020).

Shimizu K, Wharton G, Sakamoto H, et al. (2020) Resurgence of COVID-19 in Japan. *BMJ* 370: m3221.

Stewart J (2020) The subjective turn: For Hegel, human nature strives through history to unchain itself from tradition. But is such inner freedom worth the cost? *Aeon.* https://aeon.co/essays/hegel-and-the-history-of-human-nature.

Stockwin A (2020) How will COVID-19 reshape the world? *East Asia Forum.* www.eastasiaforum.org/2020/04/15/how-will-covid-19-reshape-the-world/.

Strangio S (2020) *In the Dragon's Shadow: Southeast Asia in the Chinese Century.* New Haven, CT; London: Yale University Press.

Takuma K (2020) Japan leading global health governance. *East Asia Forum.* www.eastasiaforum.org/2020/09/30/japan-leading-global-health-governance/.

Taylor S (2019) *The Psychology of Pandemics: Preparing for the Next Global Outbreak of Infectious Disease.* Cambridge: Cambridge Scholars Publishing.

Tiberghien Y (2007) *Entrepreneurial States: Reforming Corporate Governance in France, Japan, and Korea.* Ithaca, NY: Cornell University Press.

Tiberghien Y (2020) Asia's rise and the transition to a post-Western global order. In Chu Y-H and Zheng Y (eds), *Contending Views on the Decline of Western-centric World and the Emerging Global Order in the 21st Century,* pp. 357–378. London: Routledge.

Tiberghien Y, Aggarwal VK, Alexandroff A, et al. (2020) Overview: Japan's leadership in the Liberal International Order. https://sppga.ubc.ca/wp-content/uploads/sites/5/2020/07/YTet-al_Introduction_Japan_LIO_July17.pdf.

Tooze A (2018) *Crashed: How a Decade of Financial Crises Changed the World*. New York: Viking.

Urata S (2020) Reimagining global value chains after COVID-19. *East Asia Forum*. www.eastasiaforum.org/2020/07/02/reimagining-global-value-chains-after-covid-19/.

Vogel EF (2011) *Deng Xiaoping and the Transformation of China*. Cambridge, MA: Harvard University Press.

Wade R (1990) *Governing the Market*. Princeton, NJ: Princeton University Press.

Wai KS (2020) Myanmar's COVID-19 response banks on Aung San Suu Kyi. *East Asia Forum*. www.eastasiaforum.org/2020/07/31/myanmars-covid-19-response-banks-on-aung-san-suu-kyi/.

Wang G (2020) The China lesson. *East Asia Forum*. www.eastasiaforum.org/2020/04/26/the-china-lesson/.

World Bank (1993) *The East Asian Miracle*. Oxford: Oxford University Press.

Yip H (2020) Taiwan shows how to carefully snip Chinese economic ties: Facing a hostile Beijing, Taipei has been decoupling from its biggest trade partner. *Foreign Policy*. https://foreignpolicy.com/2020/07/24/taiwan-china-economic-ties-decoupling/ (accessed November 30, 2020).

Zakaria F (2020) *Ten Lessons for a Post-Pandemic World*. New York: W.W. Norton & Company.

Zhou P and Shi Z-L (2021) SARS-CoV-2 spillover events. *Science* 371(6525): 120.

Acknowledgement

COVID-19 took all of us by surprise and wreaked havoc on our plans and social life. Most of all, the virus has killed many and caused untold suffering to billions of human beings around the planet. Yet, in the midst of this pain, beacons of hope, clarity, and compassion arose. I owe a debt of gratitude to those leaders. In particular, I wish to thank Dr. Michael Osterholm, director of the Center for Infectious Disease Research and Policy (CIDRAP) at the University of Minnesota, for his extremely informative and compassionate weekly podcasts. I thank Peter Berman, director of the School of Population and Public Health at the University of British Columbia (UBC), for the inspiring working group he has been leading on institutional, organizational, and governance factors (IOGP) that explain pandemic responses (Berman, 2020), along with Max Cameron and Milind Kandlikar. Peter was the first to point out the importance of comparing COVID outcomes with the Global Health Security Index developed in 2019 by Johns Hopkins University and their partners. I thank Heidi Tworek, my colleague in History and at the School of Public Policy and Global Affairs (SPPGA), for bringing me into her project on Democratic Health Communications during COVID-19. Dr. Steven Taylor (UBC Psychiatry) taught me about the tremendous psychological impact of pandemics. Dr. Santa Ono, UBC president, dedicated great efforts to nurturing a sense of community and called attention to the mental health impact of crises like this. I also thank the many great speakers in workshops I remotely attended around the world during this year.

In British Columbia, we have been blessed with the great leadership of Dr. Bonnie Henry, provincial health officer. Dr. Bonnie Henry has inspired and led our province through dedication, honesty, compassion, and caring words: the right words at the right time. She knew the limits of what she could ask and searched for the optimal pathway to guide our province through the winter of COVID-19.

Early in my search for understanding, I was greatly inspired by a presentation made by Christiana Figueres, the former executive secretary of the United Nations Framework Convention on Climate Change (UNFCC) and one of the architects of the Paris Agreement. She urged all of us to push back against forces of hopelessness and anger. It was time to make a choice for positive action and solidarity around us. She added, slowly and clearly:

> These moments are when the backbone of who are as human beings is really tested. The core of who we are is being incredibly tested. Let us rise to that test and make sure that, as much as possible, we express gratitude for many things

in this world, and joy for having wonderful people in our life. Above all we can express support for people who really need it now.[1]

I acknowledge funding support received from the Center for Japanese Research at UBC, the Peter Wall Institute for Advanced Studies at UBC, and from the Sciences Po internship program.

I acknowledge the great research assistantship and contributions from several students. Raul Restelli (Sciences Po intern) worked with me over the autumn of 2020 to gather data and documents with great professionalism, while providing me with a witty Italian angle. Saya Soma (UBC WorkLearn student) supported events we did with the Center of Japanese Research and provided great insights and data on the Japanese situation with true brilliance. Yoojung Lee, our wonderful research assistant in the project with Heidi Tworek, helped me with insights and data on the Korean case. Jeremy Jee, my Singaporean graduate student at the University of Tokyo, helped me navigate the intricacies of Singapore's tech-savvy response to COVID-19. Discussions with participants of the student-led seminar on Taiwanese politics (led by Jackie Zhao) at UBC greatly contributed to the Taiwan section. Conversations with my PhD students and alumni also helped me greatly in this work. I thank Yingqiu Kuang, Guo Li, Parker Li, Sun Ryung Park, Yoel Kornreich, Brent Sutton, as well as the great honours students.

I also thank my students in my classes at UBC in Winter 2020–1 who all spontaneously responded to a call for joint early analysis on the unfolding COVID drama, as well as the honours students in Fall 2020 who debated the impact of COVID-19 with gusto and depth that inspired me every day. So did students at Sciences Po in late April 2020 and at Tokyo University in late fall. These conversations gave me the impetus and multiple viewpoints to write this Element.

Thank you, my wonderful students, whose energy, hopes, immense talents, and creativity inspire me every day and give meaning to my work. It has been a hard and challenging year for you, and I thank you all for your resilience and efforts. I will always be here with you.

I greatly benefited from feedback received after early presentations of this work at Stanford University, with the team of the Vice Provost International at UBC, at the Canadian International Council, and at the joint event held by the 21JPSI (21st-Century Japan Politics and Society Initiative) at the Hamilton Lugar School of Global and International Studies, Indiana University and the Brookings Institution, Center for East Asia Policy Studies.

Thank you to my wonderful and esteemed colleagues at UBC, who provide every day a great working environment and a sense of community for us all.

---

[1] Source: Christiana Figueres. April 16, 2020. Public presentation at the University of Massachusetts Boston.

Thank you also to colleagues at the Asia-Pacific Foundation of Canada and at the China Institute at the University of Alberta, who provided great venues, events, and top-notch information throughout this year.

This Element could not have taken shape without the vision and hands-on comments from three fabulous editors in the Element Series, Erin Chung, Mary-Alice Haddad, and Ben Read, as well as an anonymous reviewer who put great thoughts into improving the manuscript. Thank you also to others who gave me crucial feedback to improve and do a better job. I strive to listen to all sources and unpack forces as they are. It is always a work in progress, always humbling.

Thank you to my dear friends, who stayed in contact during this age of physical distancing. In particular, I have been truly blessed with the joyful and wise support received from Alan Alexandroff, Colin Bradford, and Brian Job.

As always, I thank my family, parents, sisters, and brothers, who are always a great backbone. They encountered great struggles in Europe during this year, but the connection remained strong between us. I thank my children, Claire and Paul, who have been navigating the rough waters of 2020 with great spirit, cheerfulness, and a sense of hope. Their music, their songs, and their words of wisdom nurtured this lonely year.

I express infinite thanks to my wife Yvonne, my sapient and mischievous COVID-19 lockdown companion, who knows how to grow seeds of hope in the midst of turmoil. Thank you for your eternal strength and love, boundless creativity, and life-long inspiration. It is not an exaggeration or a joke to admit honestly that this work and others would not be here without you.

I acknowledge that this work was written on the traditional, ancestral, and unceded territory of the Coast Salish WSANEC First Nation people, the island of SKTAK. The Coast Salish people have a painful memory about pandemics: they once suffered devastation from the diseases brought from the Old World. Their wisdom and deep understanding of our world, built on thousands of years of civilization rooted in this land, have been a great source of inspiration for me (Elliott and Poth, 1983).

As you close this Element, I invite you, my reader to pause for a moment of silence in honour of all the people who lost their lives and all who suffered untold hardships. I wish to acknowledge the extraordinary contributions of all the heroic frontline workers who sustained the rest of us during the pandemic: health-care workers, farmers, delivery workers, supermarket staff, restaurant owners and employees, packers, warehouse staff, drivers, firefighters, garbage collectors, and many others. Without you and your important work, our life stops. As noted by Michael Sandel, our society has failed to recognize that such contributions are critical to our society. We must better acknowledge and reward these workers, today and tomorrow. Real people and their families have greatly suffered throughout this pandemic and borne an unequal burden. It is the pain and efforts of people that many of us don't see that carried our society through the storm. It is our collective responsibility to do a better job as a humanity to recognize everyone.

Thank you to my wonderful community and neighbors on Mayne Island. Special thanks to our valiant post office, which became the lifeline of our livelihood and carried the flow of books that made my work possible, even though the mail boat sank in an ill-timed storm during the process. Thanks also to our hard-working hardware store and our fabulous recycling center volunteers. I am grateful for the beautiful natural environment of BC, its soaring eagles, witty otters, and mighty humpback whales and orcas. They nurtured me every day.

Here is hope for humanity to emerge from COVID-19 with new ideas and a renewed sense of mutual care. This terrible pandemic has destroyed lives, hopes, and communities and pitted neighbor against neighbor, cities against countryside, culture against culture. Humanity, for all its flaws, has the where-withal to do a better job and summon our best creative and entrepreneurial energies, rather than greed and hatred of one another. We can do better than what we did in 2020. And we can learn from the innovations and efforts of others.

Cambridge Elements ≡

Politics and Society in East Asia

Erin Aeran Chung
Johns Hopkins University
Erin Aeran Chung is the Charles D. Miller Associate Professor of East Asian Politics in the Department of Political Science at the Johns Hopkins University. She specializes in East Asian political economy, international migration, and comparative racial politics. She is the author of *Immigration and Citizenship in Japan* (Cambridge, 2010, 2014; Japanese translation, Akashi Shoten, 2012) and *Immigrant Incorporation in East Asian Democracies* (Cambridge, 2020). Her research has been supported by grants from the Academy of Korean Studies, the Japan Foundation, the Japan Foundation Center for Global Partnership, the Social Science Research Council, and the American Council of Learned Societies.

Mary Alice Haddad
Wesleyan University
Mary Alice Haddad is the John E. Andrus Professor of Government, East Asian Studies, and Environmental Studies at Wesleyan University. Her research focuses on democracy, civil society, and environmental politics in East Asia as well as city diplomacy around the globe. A Fulbright and Harvard Academy scholar, Haddad is author of *Effective Advocacy: Lessons from East Asia's Environmentalists* (MIT, 2021), *Building Democracy in Japan* (Cambridge, 2012), and *Politics and Volunteering in Japan* (Cambridge, 2007), and co-editor of *Greening East Asia* (University of Washington, 2021), and *NIMBY is Beautiful* (Berghahn Books, 2015). She has published in journals such as Comparative Political Studies, Democratization, Journal of Asian Studies, and Nonprofit and Voluntary Sector Quarterly, with writing for the public appearing in the Asahi Shimbun, the Hartford Courant, and the South China Morning Post.

Benjamin L. Read
University of California, Santa Cruz
Benjamin L. Read is a professor of Politics at the University of California, Santa Cruz. His research has focused on local politics in China and Taiwan, and he also writes about issues and techniques in field research. He is author of *Roots of the State: Neighborhood Organization and Social Networks in Beijing and Taipei* (Stanford, 2012), coauthor of *Field Research in Political Science: Practices and Principles* (Cambridge, 2015), and co-editor of *Local Organizations and Urban Governance in East and Southeast Asia: Straddling State and Society* (Routledge, 2009). His work has appeared in journals such as Comparative Political Studies, Comparative Politics, the Journal of Conflict Resolution, the China Journal, the China Quarterly, and the Washington Quarterly, as well as several edited books.

About the Series
The Cambridge Elements series on Politics and Society in East Asia offers original, multidisciplinary contributions on enduring and emerging issues in the dynamic region of East Asia by leading scholars in the field. Suitable for general readers and specialists alike, these short, peer-reviewed volumes examine common challenges and patterns within the region while identifying key differences between countries. The series consists of two types of contributions: 1) authoritative field surveys of established concepts and themes that offer roadmaps for further research; and 2) new research on emerging issues that challenge conventional understandings of East Asian politics and society. Whether focusing on an individual country or spanning the region, the contributions in this series connect regional trends with points of theoretical debate in the social sciences and will stimulate productive interchanges among students, researchers, and practitioners alike.

Cambridge Elements ☰

Politics and Society in East Asia

Elements in the series

The East Asian COVID-19 Paradox
Yves Tiberghien

A full series listing is available at: www.cambridge.org/EPEA

Printed in the United States
by Baker & Taylor Publisher Services